Harrods

A

Palace

in

Knightsbridge

HARRODS

A

PALACE

IN

KNIGHTSBRIDGE

ORIGINATED AND RESEARCHED

BY TIM DALE

PUBLISHED BY

MOHAMED AL FAYED

HARRODS
PUBLISHING

Photography by Fritz von der Schulenburg

Additional photography by Stuart Duff
Know-How text by Tiffany Daneff

With thanks to all the hard-working
Harrodians, who co-operated so cordially
in the production of this book.

First published in 1995 by
Harrods Publishing
55 Park Lane, London W1Y 3DB

Harrods Limited, Knightsbridge

British Library Cataloguing in Publication Data
A catalogue record for this book is available
from the British Library

ISBN 1 900055 01 5
Copyright © Harrods Limited, 1995

Editorial Coordinator: Christiane Sherwen
Editor: Sebastian Wormell
Design: Michael Johnson, johnson banks

Production: Deer Park Productions

Colour origination by Precise Litho Ltd, London

Printed and bound by Arnoldo Mondadori Editore, Verona, Italy

FRONTISPIECE: *In one of the store's
elegant bronze 1920s lifts stands Rodney,
the special messenger entrusted with deliveries
to Buckingham Palace.*

CONTENTS

EVERYTHING
FOR
EVERYBODY
EVERYWHERE

*The highly
ornamental central
pediment on the
Brompton Road
façade. Richly
sculptured in
Doulton's terracotta,
Britannia, seated
among nymphs
and cherubs,
above the company's
motto, 'Everything
for Everybody
Everywhere'.*

No other department store in the world looks quite like it. It is as though some vast neo-Renaissance palace had been set down among the surging traffic of Knightsbridge. Its colour alone makes it distinctive. Faced in terracotta, it is honey-coloured in the sunlight, burnt sienna in the shade. Opulently domed, turreted, pillared, pedimented and gabled, it exudes a supreme self-confidence. Its air is unashamedly grand. And, as is only to be expected of a store that has developed into an international symbol of excellence and enterprise, its skyline is alive with the fluttering flags of all nations.

Although Harrods may not be quite the biggest nor the oldest established department store in the world, it is far and away the most glamorous and distinguished. Below the statue of Britannia in the central pediment are the words *Omnia Omnibus Ubique* — 'Everything for Everybody Everywhere'. It is a motto, or rather a creed, that has been followed to an extraordinary degree.
The range and quality of merchandise and services Harrods offers is unsurpassed. The store was once able, quite justifiably, to adopt the telegraphic address of 'Everything, London'.
Such is its worldwide renown that even before the First World War Harrods could boast that, just as letters could be addressed simply to 'The King, London' or to 'The Pope, Rome', so the words 'Harrod's Stores, England' were sufficient for the international postal service.

   Harrods is not simply a famous store, it is a national institution, a by-word for the sort of thing which Britain does best. The name is synonymous with long-established superiority. When the actor and writer Dirk Bogarde chose the title *A Short Walk from Harrods* for a volume of his autobiography, it was not so much to give a geographical location or to indicate the convenience of living near a well-known shop, as to suggest a certain style of life.

   No wonder Harrods has for so long been one of the obligatory sights, one of the great tourist meccas, of London.

   Visitors are never disappointed. The interior is no less sumptuous than the exterior. Although the atmosphere of Harrods has always been luxurious, the store has undergone a transformation in recent years. The energy and imagination of the present owners have brought back the grandeur of its greatest days. Long-hidden Edwardian features have been restored to public view; newly designed departments evoke the romanticism of the past. Besides the colourful Art Nouveau tiling of the Food Halls and the elegant Art Deco fittings of the Leather Room, there are new interiors conceived with a splendour not seen since Edwardian times: the white, cream and gold elegance of the Jewellery Room and the bronze shimmer of the amazing Egyptian Hall.
Yet underlying Harrods' traditionalism is the most modern technology. Only in its restored fin de siècle décor and its sense of service is Harrods old-fashioned.

BELOW: *A letterhead bearing the reassuring telegraphic address: 'Everything Harrods London'.*
RIGHT: *The bronze Art Deco fittings in the Leather room which were restored in 1987.*

The Royal Warrants that decorate the corners of the façade show Harrods' long association with the British royal family. Since Queen Alexandra first visited the store in the early years of the century, six generations have done their shopping here. Members of foreign royal houses — kings and queens, princes and princesses — have long been among its customers.

One of the most unusual orders was placed by a queen — Queen Elisabeth of the Belgians. In 1914, when the Belgian royal family had been forced to establish itself, in the midst of the army, on the last remaining strip of unoccupied Belgian soil, the Queen was distressed at having had to abandon all the hospitals and medical supplies to the German invaders. A new, properly equipped hospital was needed immediately. There was, she decided, only one thing to do. She contacted Harrods.

Within a matter of days the equipment was on its way across the Channel, with members of Harrods staff to organize its installation, and a 640-bed hospital set up in record time. Herbert Costa, manager of the Building and Electrical Departments, later received the Cross of the Ordre de Léopold II from the grateful Belgian King.

Indeed, it is almost as much for its 'service to the world' as for the variety and quality of its goods in the store that Harrods is renowned. In the days of empire it would have moved your household effects to Karachi with as much apparent ease and efficiency as it would have delivered a couple of lamb chops to an address in Cadogan Square. The export department is still busy today. It will send an oriental rug to the orient, French wine to France; it has even, on one occasion, sent a fossil excavated in Texas and then sold at Harrods, back to Texas. It comes as no surprise to see, in a photograph taken in Venice in the 1920s, that a container being delivered by boat to a palazzo on the Grand Canal is inscribed 'Harrods Ltd'. Jessica Mitford, in her auto-biographical study *A Fine Old Conflict* gives an example of the store's varied and wide-ranging services — and the loyalty of its customers.

L.W. "SOMME."   L.W. "MEUSE."

ABOVE: *These two fetching ladies are sporting the 'Somme' and the 'Meuse' raincoats, advertised during the First World War. Women were obviously coveting their menfolk's service trenchcoats. More seriously, the store responded to the demand for a field hospital in Belgium, which they supplied and set up in 1914.*

BELOW: *Venice is not the furthest point on the globe reached by Harrods but delivery of goods there by gondola certainly takes on an exotic quality, 1929.*

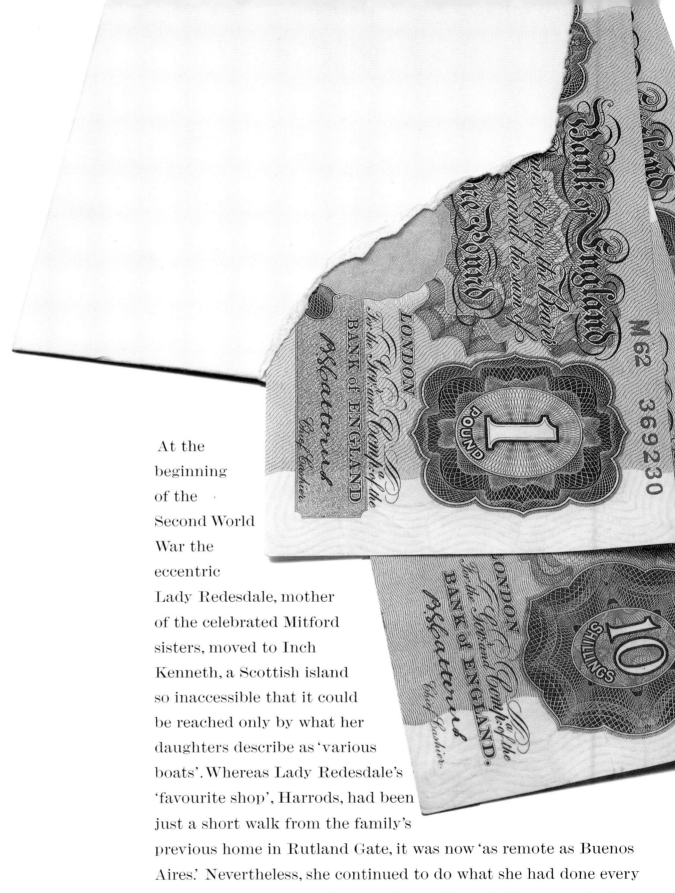

At the
beginning
of the
Second World
War the
eccentric
Lady Redesdale, mother
of the celebrated Mitford
sisters, moved to Inch
Kenneth, a Scottish island
so inaccessible that it could
be reached only by what her
daughters describe as 'various
boats'. Whereas Lady Redesdale's
'favourite shop', Harrods, had been
just a short walk from the family's
previous home in Rutland Gate, it was now 'as remote as Buenos
Aires.' Nevertheless, she continued to do what she had done every
Monday morning: send the laundry to Harrods. It was 'packed
into large wicker hampers for its weekly journey by boats, train
and van to that emporium.'

Nor did Lady Redesdale's long-distance dealings
with Harrods end there. She regularly received large, bulky
envelopes from the store. What, she was once asked, did they
contain? 'Just some new pound notes from Harrods bank,' she
answered airily, 'so much fresher than the ones you get up here.'

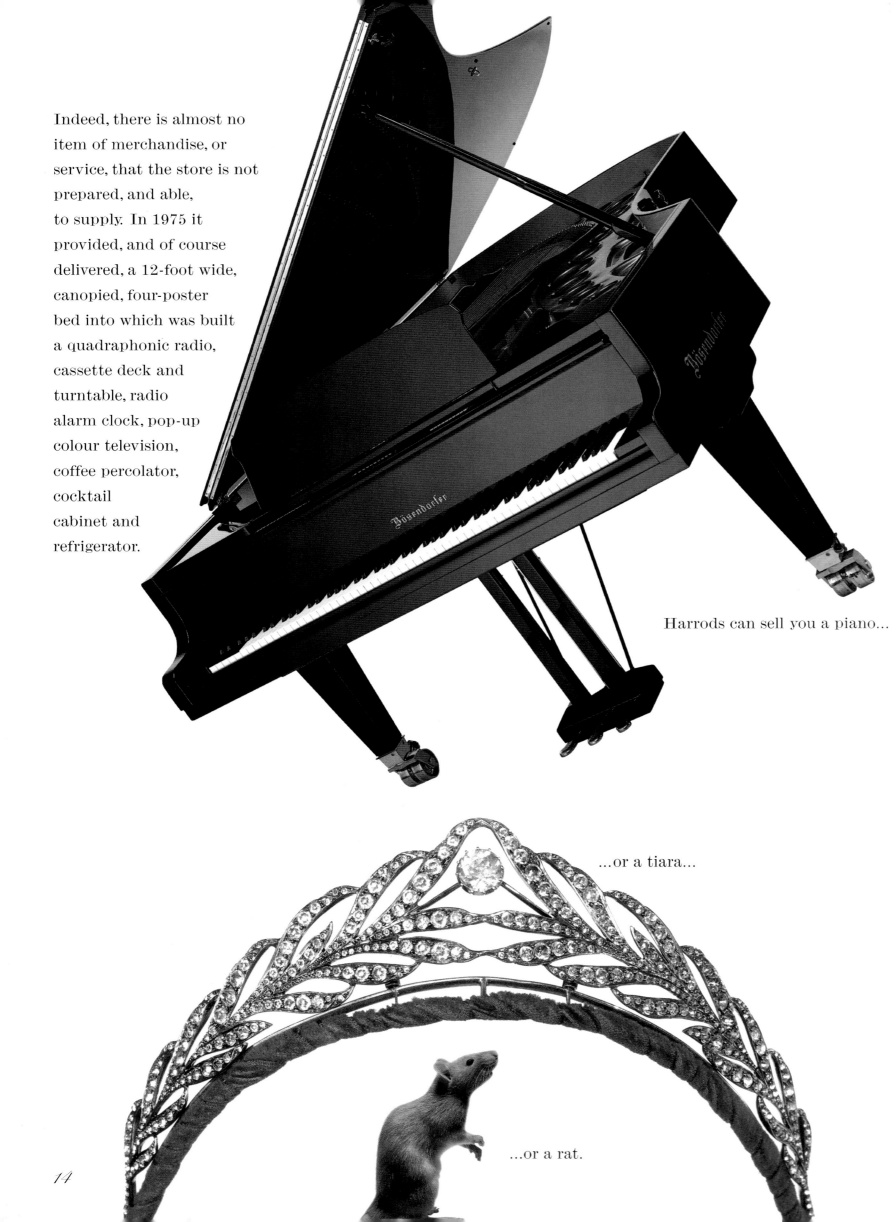

Indeed, there is almost no item of merchandise, or service, that the store is not prepared, and able, to supply. In 1975 it provided, and of course delivered, a 12-foot wide, canopied, four-poster bed into which was built a quadraphonic radio, cassette deck and turntable, radio alarm clock, pop-up colour television, coffee percolator, cocktail cabinet and refrigerator.

Harrods can sell you a piano...

...or a tiara...

...or a rat.

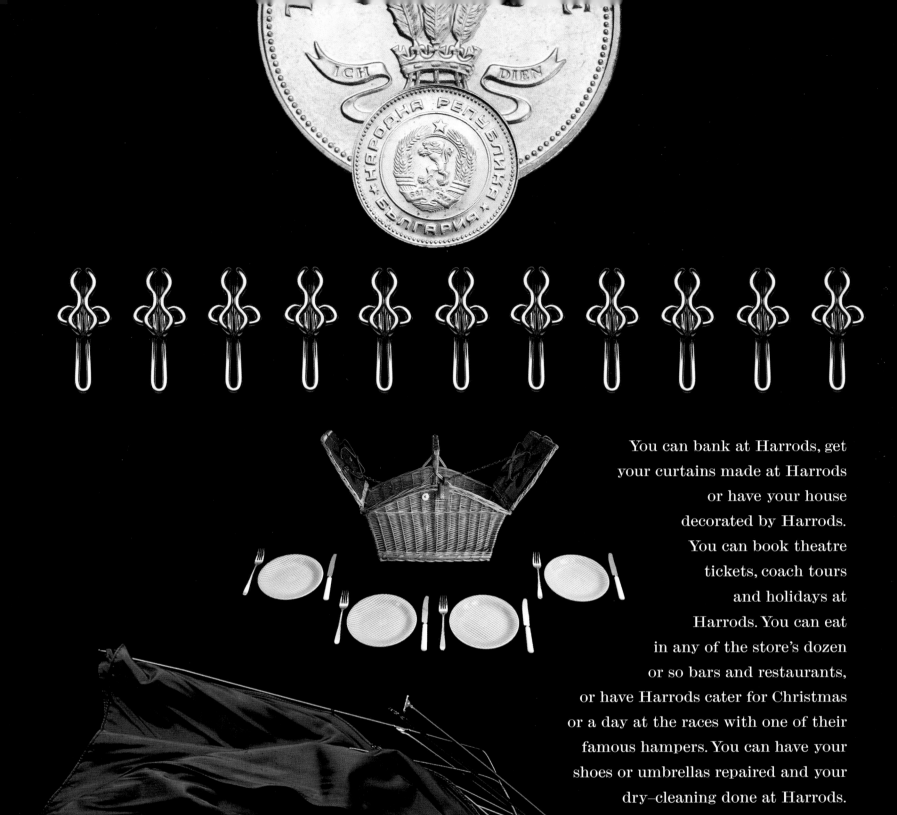

You can bank at Harrods, get your curtains made at Harrods or have your house decorated by Harrods. You can book theatre tickets, coach tours and holidays at Harrods. You can eat in any of the store's dozen or so bars and restaurants, or have Harrods cater for Christmas or a day at the races with one of their famous hampers. You can have your shoes or umbrellas repaired and your dry–cleaning done at Harrods.

Your medical prescriptions can be provided by Harrods pharmacy. You can have your spectacles made up at Harrods, and your wedding dress or your army uniform fitted.

A DAY AT HARRODS

It is often claimed that the Harrods day starts before dawn.
But it actually starts long before; in fact, it never really ends.
It would be more accurate to say that Harrods never sleeps. Even
at dead of night, there is activity in the store. In the bowels of the
building, the gigantic electrical generators thud continuously.
Seventy per cent of the store's electricity is generated in this vast
engine room. Down here it is like being in the depths of some
great ocean liner: the noise is deafening, the heat just bearable.
For 24 hours a day, for 365 days a year, this mighty heart is kept
thumping. There is always someone on duty.

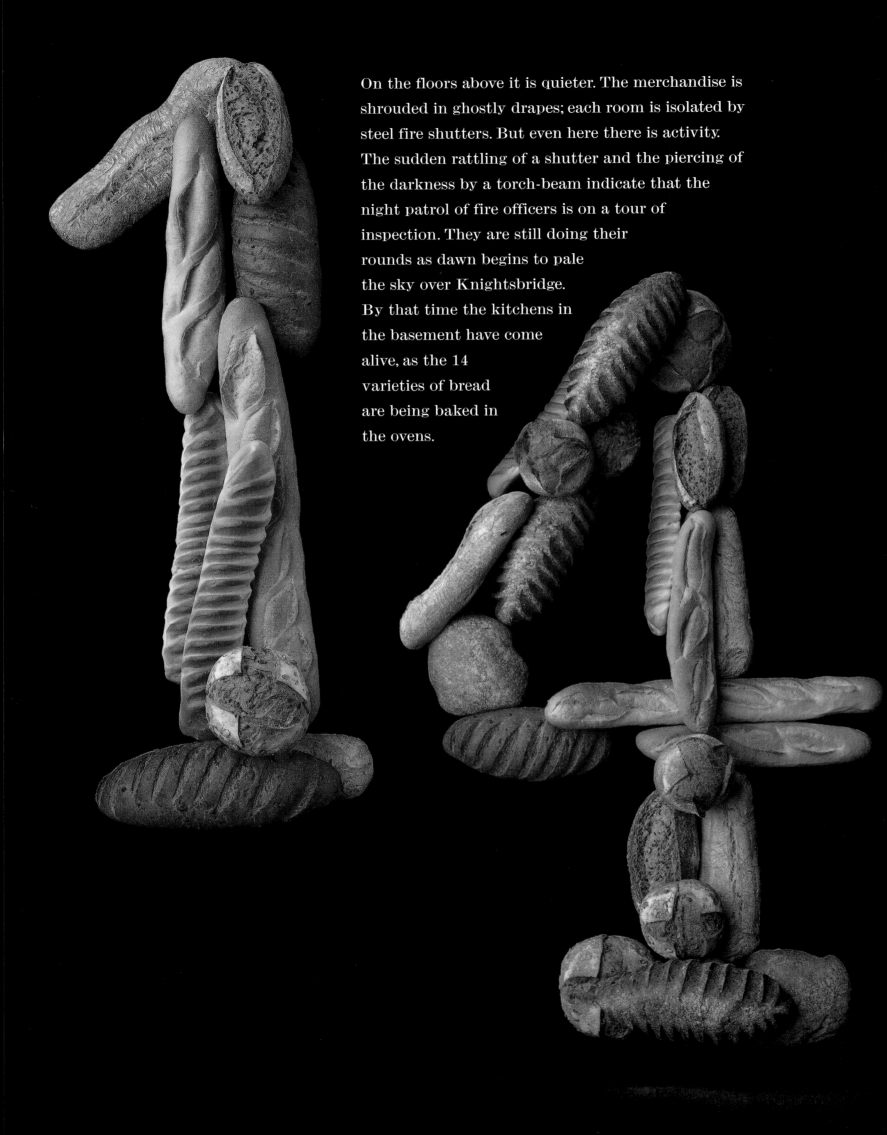

On the floors above it is quieter. The merchandise is shrouded in ghostly drapes; each room is isolated by steel fire shutters. But even here there is activity. The sudden rattling of a shutter and the piercing of the darkness by a torch-beam indicate that the night patrol of fire officers is on a tour of inspection. They are still doing their rounds as dawn begins to pale the sky over Knightsbridge. By that time the kitchens in the basement have come alive, as the 14 varieties of bread are being baked in the ovens.

By that time, too, the store's buyers are on their way to London's great produce markets. Whether it be fish, meat, fruit, vegetables or flowers, the Harrods buyers must be certain that they are being offered the best and freshest produce available. Among the clamour and glitter of Billingsgate the fish buyer is choosing the 60 or so varieties of fish stocked in his department. At Smithfield the meat buyer is ensuring that the meat is of the highest possible quality. He also makes trips to Devon for lamb, to Sussex for free-range and corn-fed poultry, and to Norfolk for turkeys.

The fish buyer arriving at Billingsgate Market at dawn, is faced not only with problems of price and quality but also of meteorology. A storm in the Indian Ocean means there will be no Red Admiral or blue Parrot fish on display that day.

OPPOSITE: *At Harrods, 14 varieties of bread – including walnut, malted grain, pumpkin, boucheron, sunflower, sultana and various kinds of baguette – baked in the store kitchens.*

By the time this produce arrives at the store, the perimeter of the building is coming to life. At the south-western corner of the shop, delivery vehicles wait their turn to unload in Hans Road. At the opposite corner, in Hans Crescent, thousands of staff members emerge from the Knightsbridge Underground station, or alight from buses to pour into the staff entrance. From here they go, by one of the store's many underground passages, into the main building itself.

Their day begins a good hour before opening time. The drapes must be removed, the float for each cash register collected from the coin centre, the jewellery taken out of the overnight safe and displayed, the fresh food from the markets unloaded from trolleys and arranged in cold cabinets or on counters, the pets fed and moved from their sleeping quarters to the Pet Shop.

In the meantime the pavements around the store are beginning to fill up with the day's first customers. They admire the no less than 75 window displays, they consult the opening times shown on the 11 doors, they check their watches. There can be few stores in the world where so many customers wait, like devout pilgrims, for the doors to open.

Once they have been let in by a smartly uniformed commissionaire, one of the ever-courteous Harrods Green Men, these early shoppers tend to head directly for some specific department. Often it is to the famous Food Halls — comprising eighteen different departments — already permeated by the delectable smells of freshly ground coffee and freshly baked bread. They are faced, not only by those 14 varieties of Harrods-baked loaves, but also by another 116 types of bread and rolls delivered each morning from bakeries all over the country.

The fish department with its colourful displays, the Fromagerie with its 350 cheeses, the tea counter with its choice of over 80 loose teas (and 32 fruit teas), the chocolates, the patisserie, the exotic fruits — all these ensure that Harrods Food Halls remain unique and that no customer will ever be disappointed. The store began as a grocer, and, as the present Chairman has said, 'Food is central to the Harrods experience.'

The Fine Jewellery Room was opened at the end of 1989. There is tight security: each entry is protected overnight by two metal screens. The security guard unveils the precious merchandise for the day.

Just as tea underpinned much of the development of the nation's trade, so it underpinned Harrods' own development. Harrods tea counter still ensures a choice of 112 varieties, including many herbal or fruit teas as well as the traditional ones.

Harrods
KNIGHTSBRIDGE

CHINA

YUNNAN GFOP

Harrods
KNIGHTSBRIDGE

CHINA

GUNPOWDER NO.1

Harrods
KNIGHTSBRIDGE

LAPSANG SOUCHONG

Harrods
KNIGHTSBRIDGE

ATED EARLGREY

Harrods
KNIGHTSBRIDGE

TARRY SOUCHONG

Harrods
KNIGHTSBRIDGE

CHINA

GRAND SZECHWAN

Harrods
KNIGHTSBRIDGE

IMPERIAL GOLD

Harrods
KNIGHTSBRIDGE

CHINA

YUNNAN KUNMING

Harrods
KNIGHTSBRIDGE

CHINA WHITE POIN

Harrods
KNIGHTSBRIDGE

RUSSIAN CARAVAN

A development in the Food Halls has been the widening of the range of prepared foods for sale. Since 1994, with the capacity of the vast new kitchens available, every national cuisine is represented. This gastronomic range is seen again in the numerous eating places within the Food Halls: the Pizzeria, the Sushi Bar, the Deli, the Champagne and Oyster Bar and the Bar Fromage.

In the Harrods Trevor Square building on the other side of
Brompton Road, the telephone exchange is dealing with those
customers who are unable to pay a personal visit. Over 10,000 calls
are received each day. Once fulfilled, orders are sent to the Dispatch
Centre and from there loaded on to the more than 50 distinctive
green and gold Harrods delivery vans. Deliveries nearer home are
often entrusted to the Harrods delivery coach: a gleaming van
driven by a liveried coachman and drawn by two of a team of eight
jet-black, high-stepping Friesian horses. These horses are stabled in
the basement of the Trevor Square building. But as they are used
on a rota system, the horses spend more of their lives on the
Chairman's country estate.

As the surge of customers increases, most are unaware of the effort and organization needed to maintain Harrods' atmosphere of unruffled elegance. Inevitably, not everything runs smoothly behind the scenes. It may be that one of the chillers in the air conditioning system is malfunctioning. The engineers discover a fault and shut the chiller down temporarily. They must move quickly to repair it since people in the departments which it serves — situated on either side of a vertical shaft

running right through the building — soon begin to notice the rising temperature. Meanwhile in the Book Department, the famous author who has come to sign copies of his latest work is taking his time over each copy, with the result that the long queue of customers waiting their turn is becoming restless. All the manager's tact is needed. If only all authors could match the briskness of Lady Thatcher, who signed a record-breaking 950 copies during her visit to the store to launch her memoirs in 1993.

The store's ever-vigilant security force has been told that a shoplifting gang is operating on the first floor. It is certain that at least one of them will be caught and handed over to the Chelsea police.

A potentially more serious situation threatens when the Director of Security receives a bomb warning. This is when, sitting alone in his basement bunker, he must make a decision: either he dismisses it as a hoax (which it usually is) or he sets off the alarm and institutes a search. To those members of the staff who experienced the Harrods bomb outrages of the past, the storewide search — despite its attendant upheavals — is always the more reassuring option.

Celebrity authors at Harrods.
TOP LEFT: Luciano Pavarotti.
BELOW LEFT: Housewife and megastar, Dame Edna Everage, alias Barry Humphries, signing his autobiography in 1989 with bridesmaid, Madge, in attendance.
BELOW: Margaret Thatcher's stamina was phenomenal: 950 signatures achieved at her 1993 book launch.

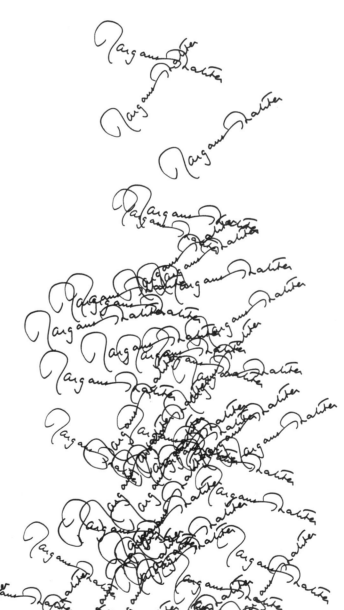

A valuable brooch has been handed in by a member of staff. How can the owner be traced? The only information the Director of Security has to go on is that it was made by Cartier. A phone call to Cartier and a search through the firm's records reveals that the piece was sold some thirty years before to a woman living in Cadogan Square. Meticulous sleuthing unearths the information that she has since moved to Ireland and is now married to a well-known racehorse-trainer. The Director of Security contacts a former senior executive of Harrods who has good connections with the horse-racing fraternity; without too much difficulty he is able to track down the address, and a few days later a delighted and incredulous customer is reunited with her brooch. It is all part of the Harrods service.

*The Georgian Restaurant was
first established at Harrods in
1911. It underwent its last
restoration in 1994.
The Georgian seats 350 people
and caters for those who enjoy a
traditional atmosphere.
It is the largest department store
restaurant in Europe.*

New Production Kitchens were opened in the sub-basement in 1994. The kitchens produce 8000 covers per day, catering for most of the seventeen restaurants in the building including the staff restaurant. They also supply bread and cakes to the Bakery, dishes for the Traiteur and fish departments and, in season, for the picnic hamper service.

Equally gratifying is the Customer Service Bureau's resolution of the problem of a Japanese woman who speaks no English but who wants to go shopping for furnishing fabrics. One of the Japanese-speaking interpreters who work on the information desks is summoned. She accompanies the woman on what turns out to be — for both customer and store — an extremely satisfactory shopping expedition.

Throughout the day the store's many restaurants and snack bars are busy. In the hour or so before lunch, activity in the kitchens is frantic; the Head Chef checks and re-checks the fare, from the gallons of soup with which the meal might start to the heaps of profiteroles with which it might end. The stylish 350-seater Georgian Restaurant on the fourth floor is the largest in-store restaurant in Europe. The staff restaurant holds the record for serving more meals than any other in Europe. Tea time is hardly less busy. The famous Harrods cream teas mean a pot of tea and as many cream cakes as one can manage.

In a department store whose daily takings average £1.5 million, trade is, of course, continuous. True to its motto, Harrods caters for everyone — not only for the denizens of 'the tiara triangle' around Knightsbridge (a diamond necklace is currently on sale for £546,000), but also for the passing shopper who has come in for a tube of toothpaste. The store will happily sell one cup, without obliging the customer to buy its matching saucer, to replace a breakage.

*The novelist Saki referred to Harrods as 'one of those places where everyone is so kind and sympathetic and devoted that one almost hates to take even a reel of cotton away from such pleasant surroundings'.
The Harrods China department is understanding about such sensitivity so, unlike other stores, will allow you to buy a cup without the saucer.*

All day a kaleidoscopic mixture of shoppers swirls through the store — asking directions, marvelling at the decor and, inevitably, spending money. Many are tourists, paying a once-in-a-lifetime visit to the world's most famous department store; others are long-established customers to whom Harrods has become a part of life. There are Middle-Eastern visitors buying jewelled watches, American businessmen booking theatre tickets, genteel old ladies up from the country choosing lavender water. Invariably, as the store closes there are customers who will ask plaintively, 'Are you closing *already*?' Patiently, cheerfully and always politely, they are ushered out.

Hardly has the clamour of the shoppers died down than it is replaced by another sound: the hum of a hundred vacuum cleaners as the small army of cleaners takes over for the next three hours. The staff trail home through the staff entrance in Hans Crescent, leaving those on 'late till' to cash up, count the day's takings and bank the proceeds in the coin centre. By 9 p.m. the cleaners are finishing their work; an hour later the men who have been painting a ceiling pack up and go. The engine room is reduced to minimum power and, at 11 p.m., the fifteen thousand light bulbs that so spectacularly illuminate the outside of the building are switched off. The silent, shrouded, shuttered store belongs to the firemen once more.

Perhaps one of them, as he patrols the Room of Luxury on the ground floor, flashes the beam of his torch on to the piles of sumptuous merchandise, bearing the most famous designer names in the world. He almost certainly does not realise that he is standing near the spot where, a century and a half ago, Charles Henry Harrod served behind the counter of his simple little grocery shop.

'The most convenient place in the World for Shopping', a Harrods advertisement of 1898 produced this modest claim. No doubt confirmed by the 50,000 people who pass through Harrods daily, from door opening at 10 a.m. until sometimes 8 at night. Some come only to look at this famous tourist attraction, but those who buy have a chance to savour a world of calm service where the sales assistants are both interested and knowledgeable.

5 Clarkson Mrs Mary, lodging house
6 Medlicott Edward Hardwick, esq

Mid. Queen's bldgs. *Brompton,*
Queen's blds. Bromp. to Up. Queen's blds.
2 Genet Fredk. Jas. surgeon
3 Wickens Edwin, cheesemonger
4 Garrard Rev. George
5 Whitefield Thos. surgeon & chemist
6 Solomon Michael, potato dealer
7A, Weale William Allen, bootmaker
7 Johnson Benj. Barton, cheesemonger
8 Burden Philip Henry, grocer
9 Davis Abraham, china dealer
10 Haslam Joseph, silk mercer
11 Gasson John, academy
13 Ball Richard, mason
13 Summers Misses Elizabeth & Su-
sannah, milliners
14 Scarnell Joseph, linendraper
15 Doughty Thomas Neale, solicitor
16 Bridgeman Misses Eliz. & Maria,
staymakers
16 Soule Cornelius, milliner
17 Jobbins Henry, baker

Middle row, *Bethnal green.*
See Green st. Bethnal green.

Middle row, 29 *Goswell st.*
2 Cherry John, carman

Middle row, 327 *High Holborn.*

2

THE HARRODS

FOUNDING

A LEGEND

Middle Queen's Buildings in Brompton Road, from a London street directory of 1851. Charles Henry Harrod already had a financial interest in Philip Burden's grocery shop at No. 8, and was soon to take over the business.

Today Harrods presides magnificently over one of London's finest shopping streets, but the area was very different in 1849, the twelfth year of Queen Victoria's reign. The hamlet of Knightsbridge — the name comes from the old bridge which used to span the little Westbourne River near what is now Albert Gate — had once been a popular picnic spot for Londoners. Now the fields and market gardens were disappearing under bricks and mortar. But the little squares and terraced houses along the turnpike road which led to Fulham by way of the village of Brompton, had none of the stuccoed grandeur of nearby Belgravia.

The big cavalry barracks on the edge of Hyde Park brought some life to the district. Officers of the Life Guards kept their mistresses in the discreet little houses of Trevor Square, and along the 'Brompton Road', as the turnpike road was known (though the name became official only in 1863), some of the houses were converted into shops. But it was hardly a shopping street. Looking back at the end of the century, an inhabitant remembered 'only a few primitive places of business on the southern side, facing Brompton Row, and then private houses standing back in long gardens'.

It was probably in 1849 that Charles Henry Harrod first established a financial interest in one of these businesses, a struggling grocery shop run by a certain Philip Henry Burden at 8 Middle Queen's Buildings, near the Knightsbridge end of the Brompton Road. Harrod was an Essex man, born the son of a miller in Lexden near Colchester in 1799. After his marriage to Elizabeth Digby, from the nearby village of Birch, the couple had moved to London, and in 1833 Harrod opened a shop dealing in tea and groceries in Cable Street, Stepney. Its success eventually led to the opening, in 1849, of a wholesale business in Eastcheap, which at that time was the centre of London's tea and grocery trade. Philip Burden was one of Harrod's customers and the two men became friends. When Harrod realised that Burden was in financial difficulties, he offered to help, at first by paying Burden's shop rent without pressing for repayment and then by involving himself ever more closely in the running of the business.

Victorian grocer and tea-merchant Charles Henry Harrod (1799-1885), the founder of Harrods, photographed in retirement. Most big stores developed from draper's shops; to begin as a grocer's was unusual.

The little shop Harrod acquired in Brompton Road occupied only a tiny part of the massive frontage of Harrods today.

A replica of the original grocery shop was built in Harrods Central Exhibition Hall when the store celebrated its centenary in 1949.

It was not until 1853, after Burden had decided to give up his shop and emigrate, that Harrod and his family — his wife and four sons — moved from the East End to live above the shop. Concern for his family's health was probably the main reason for the move, particularly after the cholera epidemic that had ravaged the City in 1848 and 1849. The air of Knightsbridge was healthier than the smoky East End, and the open space of Hyde Park was nearby.

Charles Henry Harrod was already in his mid-fifties and looking forward to retirement. He soon disposed of his premises in Cable Street and Eastcheap, but he had no ambitious plans for his new shop. He was not to know that he would bequeath his name to the most famous department store in the world.

In 1853 the shop gave little indication of its brilliant destiny. It was no more than a one-room, flat-roofed extension built over what had been the front garden of the terraced house. Across a single counter, standing on a sawdust-strewn floor, Charles Henry Harrod sold groceries including, of course, tea, which was then the most important single item provided by grocers. He was helped by two assistants and an errand boy. Estimates of his weekly takings vary, but they may have risen from around £3 to £20 during the first decade.

The owner's gradually improving commercial fortunes were offset by domestic sorrows. In 1854 one of his sons died, followed six years later by his wife, Elizabeth. In 1861, at the

the age of sixty-two, Harrod decided to retire, and instead of handing the shop over to his eldest son, Charles Digby Harrod, he sold it to him for £500. This meant that the father was able to divide his fortune among his other sons. (One of them, William Digby Harrod emigrated to New Zealand, while the other, Henry Digby Harrod, was to set up his own grocery shop in Old Compton Street, Soho.)

As far as Charles Digby Harrod was concerned, his £500 could not have been better spent.

CHARLES DIGBY HARROD

Charles Digby Harrod was just twenty when he took over his father's little shop. Although young, he was not really a novice: since the age of sixteen he had been working for the grocers Read, Warren and Harrison in the City. He brought with him energy, efficiency and ambition: he was determined to build up the business. To show who was now in charge he formally dismissed and then re-engaged his father's two assistants. By present-day standards Harrod's regime was strict: employees were fined for lateness, and they could be sacked at a moment's notice. But the young 'guv'nor' never expected his staff to do anything that he was not prepared to do himself. He may have been a disciplinarian but he was always fair.

Characteristically, it was not until Charles Digby Harrod had paid off his father that he married. His bride, the daughter of another grocer, was a local Sunday school teacher named Caroline Godsmark. By 1864 the couple were established in the house behind the shop, which had been redesignated 105 Brompton Road.

In the following decades the district was to change out of all recognition. The Great Exhibition of 1851, held in Joseph Paxton's glittering Crystal Palace next to Knightsbridge Barracks in Hyde Park and visited by tens of thousands, had been a turning point in the fortunes of this part of London. In 1862 another great International Exhibition, held where the Natural History

ABOVE: *Charles Digby Harrod (1841-1905), who turned his father's grocery shop into a department store.*
BELOW: *Since 1921 the houses in Trevor Square have been dwarfed by Harrods factory and warehouse building.*
OPPOSITE: *Detail of a 'Balloon View of London', 1851. Harrod's shop was in the street marked Brompton Row (now Brompton Road), in the block between New Street (now Hans Crescent) and Queen Street (now Hans Road). In the foreground is Hyde Park, with the Crystal Palace and the cavalry barracks.*

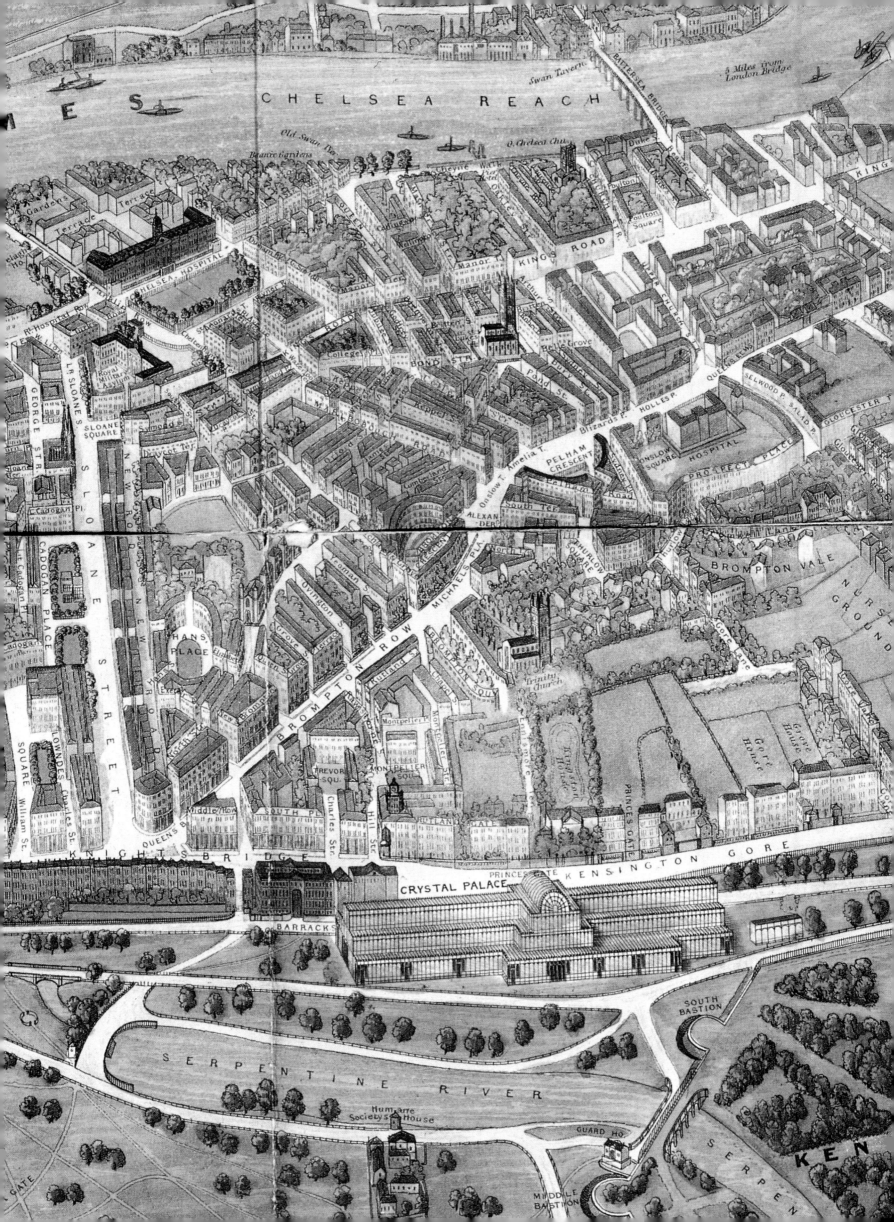

LEFT: *Blending and grinding at the coffee counter in the tea and coffee department, enlarged and refurbished in 1994. For Victorian grocers such as Charles Henry Harrod, tea, and to a lesser extent coffee, were of great importance; Harrods still gives them prominence today.*
ABOVE: *Coffee tin from the 1920s.*

Museum now stands, again attracted thousands of visitors. Brompton Road was widened to provide access and became now one of the busiest highways of the metropolis. Following the exhibitions, great museums and institutes sprang up to create a new 'city of palaces' south of the park, which was to transform the neighbourhood. Nevertheless, even in the 1870s Knightsbridge still had a slightly raffish reputation and many of the back-streets were insanitary slums. The omens, however, were good.

'CO-OPERATIVE PRICES'

Harrod was young and good-looking and knew how to charm his lady customers. But to survive and expand his business he also needed courage to fight two important battles. The first was against long established and costly practices: the payment of bribes, known as 'cooks' perks', to servants of households in order to keep their valuable custom, and the granting of extended credit terms, sometimes lasting for years. Charles Digby Harrod insisted on immediate payment, in full and in cash. His boldness paid off: he was able to lower his prices and attract more customers.

Harrod's second major battle was against the co-operative movement, which arrived in London in the 1860s. The Civil Service Supply Association and the Civil Service Co-operative Society, and later the Army and Navy Co-operative Society, sold groceries and other merchandise at discount prices to customers who paid a small membership subscription. They soon grew into large establishments selling a wide range of goods — in fact London's first department stores.

The resourceful Charles Harrod faced this competition head-on. He was able to offer low prices without requiring membership, and under the challenging headline 'Co-operative Prices', began advertising in the press. His first advertisement appeared in the *Pall Mall Gazette* in 1866. It offered, among other items, seven pounds of rice for one shilling.

FROM GROCER'S SHOP TO DEPARTMENT STORE

The shop was by now taking between £200 and £250 a week, and Harrod decided that the time had come for further expansion. His staff was increased to five, and in 1868 his cousin, William Kibble, was brought in to help. Kibble was to remain with the store for the next sixty years. He had a particular expertise in fruit and vegetables, and the store was soon renowned for the freshness and excellence of its produce. It is a reputation that Harrods has maintained ever since.

By 1867 a new plate glass window had been installed; but there were no window displays, just wire blinds lettered with the words 'C.D. Harrod, Grocer'.

The business may have been flourishing but there remained that perennial retailer's problem — the need for more space. Charles Harrod solved it by moving house. With his wife and three daughters (he was to have six more children) he moved to Esher in Surrey. He could now use the whole of 105 Brompton Road for the shop: the ground floor kitchen and parlour were converted into storage areas, and the whole of the original shop space, plus the first floor of the house, was now used for selling. New lines — patent medicines, perfumery and stationery — were entrusted to William Kibble. This expansion was significant: it marked the beginning of the transformation of a simple grocery shop into a department store.

By 1871 — ten years after taking over the business — Charles Digby Harrod was firmly established. His takings had risen to £1000 a week. Although he had now to come up to London each morning by train

William Kibble photographed wearing his jaunty holiday cap, at Aberystwyth, 1903. He was C.D. Harrod's cousin and joined the staff in 1868, when the shop started to sell fruit and vegetables. Junior staff remembered him as a fearsome disciplinarian. By the time he retired in 1917, he had seen Harrods transformed.
BELOW: *Kibble would have difficulty recognizing some of the exotic produce selected by Harrods' fruit and vegetable buyer for the sophisticated shopper of today.*

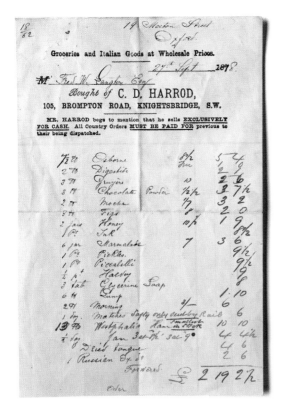

A bill from 1878, for groceries to be delivered to an out-of-town customer at Merton Street, Oxford. According to the printed heading, Harrod offered his wares 'at Wholesale Prices', and immediate payment in cash was required.

he was always in the shop by six. In shirtsleeves, with a billycock hat firmly on his head, he would be there to greet his sixteen employees. These included two aproned lads who delivered goods by basket or handcart. It was only in 1876 that the business acquired a single horse-drawn van.

Harrod's practical character and straightforward business methods are evident in his catalogues and invoices. The first of his catalogues, published in 1870, declared that his goods were offered 'at the lowest possible prices for Nett Cash'. His bills carried the uncompromising warning that 'MR. HARROD begs to mention that he sells EXCLUSIVELY FOR CASH. All country orders MUST BE PAID FOR previous to their being dispatched.' But as one of his employees remembered, 'He had his generous side, and many of our poor customers who had exhausted their weekly wages with us would often get a little extra at his expense.'

The 1870s saw a further enlargement of the shop's premises. The small back garden disappeared under a two-storey extension. The second floor now contained the counting house — to which 'cash boys' had to run whenever change was needed.

In 1874 he acquired from his neighbour, Stewart the milliner, the leases of numbers 101 and 103 Brompton Road adjoining his premises on the east. With three houses now at his disposal, Harrod could stock many additional lines: cooked meats, confectionery, china and flowers. By 1880 he was employing a hundred people and on the blinds there appeared, for the first time, 'HARROD'S STORES'.

THE GREAT FIRE OF 1883

Renovations in progress in 1883 probably caused the disastrous fire which swept through the store on the night of 6 December. A workman may have left a candle burning in the basement, or a window left ajar may have caused a curtain to be blown against a gas jet. The store — packed with additional Christmas merchandise — was soon ablaze. Gearing, the dispatch manager, who lived nearby, was wakened. He rushed to Brompton Road, where he was greeted, in the words of the *Chelsea Herald*,

…by a scene of splendidly terrible character. Only the skeleton of three large shops and the stores at the base remained, but the fire raged in a seething mass, shooting high up in the air from the inner portion, whilst the flames clung tenaciously to the window frames, mouldings and other woodwork, thus outlining the structure as if by an intentional illumination. The steam fire engine and hose from the hydrants were pouring tons of water upon the burning mass with no apparent effect …

The shocked Gearing sent another Harrod's employee to fetch the 'guv'nor'. By this time Harrod and his family had moved to Sydenham and it was from here, in a hansom cab, that he came hurrying to Knightsbridge. When he reached it, in the grey light of the winter's dawn, Harrod's Stores was a smoking ruin. Damage was estimated at between £30,000 and £50,000.

Resolute as ever, Harrod took charge of the situation. He established headquarters nearby from where he issued orders to his demoralised staff. On that very morning — 7 December 1883 — he sent a letter to each of his regular customers. For calm in the face of adversity it could hardly be bettered. 'I greatly regret to inform you,' it read, 'that, in consequence of the above premises being burnt down, your order will be delayed in the execution a day or two. I hope, in the course of Tuesday or Wednesday next, to be able to forward it. In the meantime may I ask you for your kind indulgence.' It was signed, 'your obedient servant, C.D. Harrod.'

But how, exactly, was the promise to be fulfilled? Apparently, Harrod was helped by a man who was to play an important part in the future of the store. It seems that Charles Digby Harrod had first met him the year before, on an omnibus. According to one version of the story, Harrod had found himself without money for the fare, and had to seek assistance from the

ABOVE: *The fire which destroyed the shop on the night of 6 December 1883 was a disaster — the entire Christmas stock was lost. This drawing made in 1949 recalls the catastrophe.*
BELOW: *Press reports gave dramatic accounts of the conflagration.*
OPPOSITE: *Calmness in adversity: customers' orders would be delayed only 'a day or two'. A reconstruction of the letter Harrod sent out immediately after the fire.*

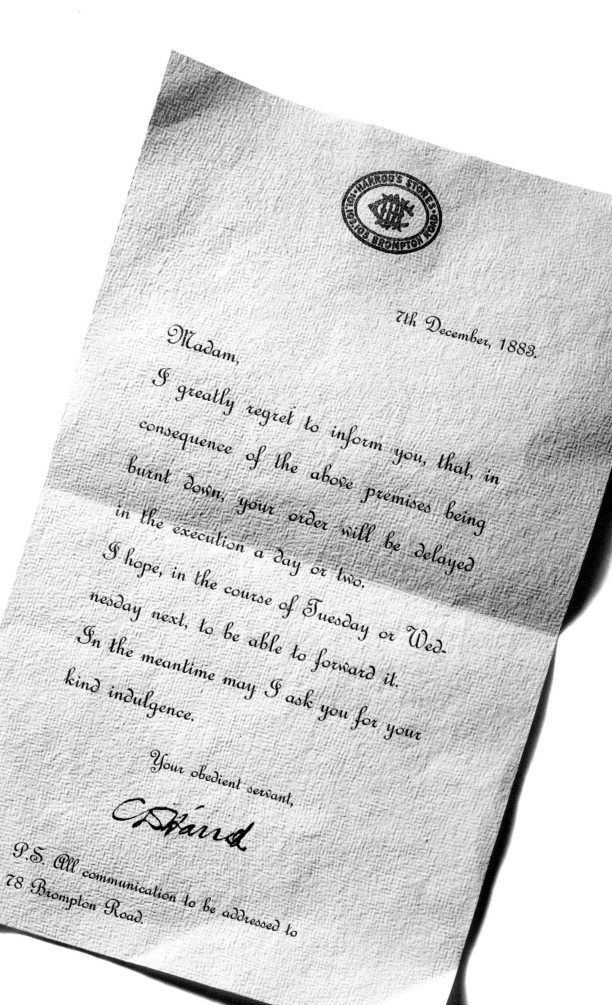

7th December, 1883.

Madam,

I greatly regret to inform you, that, in consequence of the above premises being burnt down, your order will be delayed in the execution a day or two.

I hope, in the course of Tuesday or Wednesday next, to be able to forward it.

In the meantime may I ask you for your kind indulgence.

Your obedient servant,

C. D. Harrod

P.S. All communication to be addressed to 78 Brompton Road.

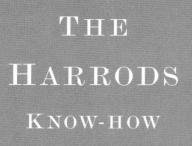
Buying antiques can be an uncertain and intimidating business, but at Harrods you can be certain, not only that you will receive a warm welcome and friendly advice, but that every piece will be of the finest quality.

Harrods, which for many years was the only British department store to sell antiques, today specializes in English and French furniture and clocks from 1851 to 1910. It is a leading supplier of pieces dating from the Sheraton Revival, an increasingly popular period known for the high quality of its decorative work.

Each piece — be it an exquisite English 1880, hand-painted satinwood card-table or a fabulously detailed French glazed ormolu and champlevé enamel mantel clock — will have been personally examined and vetted by the Harrods buyer, who spends several days a week visiting the provincial auction rooms. It will then be restored to its original condition. Chairs and sofas are taken apart in order to replace the animal glues which will have perished. Gilding and marquetry is repaired and pieces are re-upholstered and re-covered. All clocks are fully overhauled by the store's own horologist and sold with a year's guarantee. Every piece of furniture sold is accompanied by a letter of authenticity. Bearing in mind that many customers will be looking for more than one piece, the buyer has assembled a collection of furniture and ornaments that complement each other. These include French gilded hall mirrors, elegant salon paintings and handmade needlework cushions.

With a very high turnover, stock is constantly changing, so there is always something new to interest the department's regular customers, who will sometimes ask the buyer to look out for a particular piece at auction.

The antiques department has its own delivery service to ensure that all furniture is not only handled but installed by experts. They have been known to spend half a day moving furniture around to find the best position for the new piece.

the perfect antique

Nowhere will you find as large a range of china and glass as at Harrods, which is no doubt why these departments on the second floor are so popular with the modern bride. Here, in seven large rooms, are displayed a range of china that encompasses popular everyday earthenwares, from the traditional blue-and-white striped Cloverleaf to the finest hand-painted and hand-gilded porcelain.

While Harrods prides itself on offering a wide selection of traditional British ware with such famous names as Royal Doulton, Wedgwood, Spode, Royal Worcester and Minton, it also embraces and encourages, innovative designers like Emma Bridgewater, whose spongeware designs have made her a new household name.

Earthenware and stoneware services are popular for everyday oven-to-table use. These are available in a wide range of patterns, many of which have been designed for Harrods and are exclusive to the store. For a more formal dinner service, brides will often choose English fine bone china or the increasingly popular exotic designs from Italy, France and Germany, such as Richard Ginori's colourful Italian fruits.

One of the most remarkable and delightful china factories in the world is the Hungarian firm of Herend. Since it was founded in 1826, it has created over 360 different patterns, none of which has been discontinued. The changes in the political climate have meant that the factory no longer receives state subsidies, with the result that there are now long waiting-lists. To avoid this problem, Harrods stocks only six designs – delicate floral patterns, butterflies and fruits – in very large quantities, so that customers can be sure of obtaining pieces quickly.

Staff are always pleased to give advice on selecting the service that will best suit the customer's needs, and orders can be taken for special commissions, such as cresting, motifs and services in particular colours or patterns.

the perfect china

THE

HARRODS

KNOW-HOW

man sitting beside him. The stranger obliged with half a
sovereign and, on reading the business card which Harrod had
handed him as a guarantee, gave him his own card: he was
Edgar Cohen, of Messrs. I. & M. Cohen, Sponge Importers.
The punctilious Charles Digby Harrod returned the money
the following day. (A slightly different account of the meeting is
given by Cohen's daughter. According to her, Harrod was the
benefactor, paying the penny bus fare for Cohen, who had no
change smaller than a sovereign in his pocket.)

The two must have kept in touch, and on the
morning after the fire it was Cohen that Harrod contacted to
ask if he could possibly help. Unhesitatingly, Cohen came hurrying
over to Knightsbridge and lent a hand with a temporary
reorganization of the business. With the Christmas orders to
be fulfilled, goods were bought in from other stores and given
Harrod's labels (Harrod had started selling groceries with
his own label in 1880). A dozen hansom cabs were hired to carry
orders to the suppliers. Within four days, Humphrey's Hall,
a corrugated-iron building just opposite the burnt-out stores,
which had recently housed a popular Japanese exhibition,
was taken over and turned into temporary premises. As a result
of this feverish activity, every single order was filled. Christmas
1883 turned out to be the best year for trade, to date.

A NEW BUILDING

The fire had been a disaster, but the publicity had done Harrod's
Stores no harm — quite the reverse. And there was also the
opportunity to erect a new, purpose-built store. Rebuilding began
almost immediately and in September 1884 the premises were
opened for business. The shop had no architectural pretensions
and it could not compare in scale with London's big new
department stores — the Army & Navy in Victoria Street or
William Whiteley's vast emporium in Westbourne Grove — but,
for Knightsbridge at the time, its dimensions were impressive.
The shop front along the Brompton Road was still only one storey
high, but it now measured over 180 feet. The rest of the premises
now extended far back from the street and boasted a basement,
ground level and three upper floors. There was an increasingly
wide range of departments and a staff of two hundred. The most
notable feature was a grand central staircase, wide enough for
three generously-bustled ladies to ascend side by side.

ABOVE: *Edgar Cohen (right),
photographed with his brother.
The sponge importer and entrepreneur
helped Charles Digby Harrod in
the chaos after the 1883 fire.*
OPPOSITE: *A street directory of 1889,
just before Harrod sold up and Cohen
organized the flotation of the business.*
INSET: *Harrod's Store as rebuilt
in 1884 (photograph c. 1892).
Behind the relatively narrow frontage,
the store extended far
back along Queen's Gardens.*

n dentist	81 Moore Brothers, tea dealers	243
rs	83 Bush Arthur, chemist	245
estaurant	85 Green & Co. china dealers	247 &
street..	..... *here is New street.*.....	...h
Mrs. Jane	87 Turner Jonas & Son, bootmakers	251
	89 Barnes Mrs. Emma, oil & col. warho	
coffee rms	91 Sykes John & Co. cheesemongers	
rs	93 & 95 Watson Geo. F. & Co. lindrprs	**Bro**
o.builders	97 Foster Thos. & Co. wine merchnts	
glass wa	99 Pring William, fruiterer	**ton**
Mary B.	**101, 103 & 105 Harrod Charles Digby, grocer &c**	
	107 & 109 De Coster Cornelius, linen draper	1 *Lo*
Co		
tings Co.	*..here are Queen's gardens..*	2 A
, man.),	111 *The Buttercup,* Sinclair & Sinclair	3 R
	113 Clarke Arthur James, hosier	4 Cl
nralogst	115 Lilley & Skinner, bootmakers	5 St
dressma	117 Grant Brothers, tailors	6 A
ool depôt	119 Blackbeard John, linendraper	7 B
auctionr	121 Cox William, butcher	8 Se
Mutual	123 Inglis William, baker	9 M
riety,	125 Gow John I	&
rfield, sec	127 Atkinson Ge	
t. dentist	129 Ager Thom	6 H
importer	131 & 133 Turpin	7 Po
	135 Simons Mrs.	A
l carriers	..... *here is*	
ldgng. ho	137 Bocock	
er	139 & 141 Wi	
akers	143 Hughes	
of births	145 Walton,	P
re dealer	wareho	
	147 Lacy & C	

First floor: silverware, hardware, saddlery, 'modern brass goods, comprising high class fenders, fire-irons, coal boxes, . . . kitchen requisites and turnery'.

Grand staircase 'wide enough for 5 or 6 persons to ascend or descend abreast'.

Third floor: furniture, 'iron and brass bedsteads and bedding, suited for high, low, rich, or poor'.

Second floor: perfumery and cosmetics, 'a portion of the building that is sure to find favour with the gentler sex', and patent medicines.

Wines and spirits, tea and groceries: 'tins of biscuits, breeches' paste, blanc-mange, glycerine, lobsters, plate powder, sugar candy, boot top powder, wax vestas, salt, prawns, phosphor paste . . .'.

Basement, with strong-rooms, storage cellars, and 'tea rooms piled high with chests from the lowly "mixed at two shillings per pound" to the aristocratic "scented pekoe"'.

Fruit and flowers: 'daily supplies of shrubs and blooming plants, . . . the beaux' and belles' requirements in the shape of bouquets and "button holes"'.

HARRODS 1884

(as described in the *Chelsea Herald*).

Poultry and game, 'cheese from America and the foreign Gruyère, Chapzugar Camembert, with the delicious productions of Wilts . . . hams from York, Ireland, Canada or Westphalia'.

Stables 'where there are stalls and boxes for a large number of horses, together with standing room for carts, vans and hand-trucks in endless variety'.

Circulating Library

Fitting Room

Safe Deposit

One of the lifts

Typical Stairway

Telephone Order Room

Spirit Cellars

An Entrance

Gramophone Room

*Harrods in **1909**, after the great rebuilding programme of the 1890s and 1900s (from an illustrated booklet). Some of these features can still be seen today. The store erected by C.D.Harrod in 1884 did not compare with this in scale or luxury, but for its time it was impressive.*

Harrods Bakery

The correspondent of the *Chelsea Herald* could hardly contain his excitement on being faced by Harrod's wealth of merchandise on the new premises:

> *…follow our example, take nothing for granted but go and judge for yourselves, flock there in your hundreds, and thousands, nay millions if it so please you on Tuesday next, lounge round the place, particularly visit the show on the first floor, and when your tour of inspection is completed, take a price list home with you, compare it with the one issued by the Rifle and Rudder Supply Company [a humorous nickname for the Army & Navy Stores], and then if you will find all we have said to be as true as we believe it to be, you will make your way again to the Brompton Road, and your second visit will no doubt be as interesting to Mr C. D. Harrod as your first will have been to yourselves.*

Harrod's circle of customers was widening considerably; the *Chelsea Herald* could claim that his business 'which was at one time a purely local one, is now world-wide, and his clients — or customers — rank from the "Peer to the peasant"'.

In his new building Harrod did away with the old system of 'cash boys' running up to the counting house for every transaction. Instead, he took the innovative step of installing cash desks on the ground floor, so that the customers had to collect their own change, and the 'cash boys' could be released for other duties.

If Harrod had had his way, he would have continued to sell his goods on a strictly cash-only basis, with payment before delivery. However, he was eventually persuaded, by the senior members of his staff, Kibble and Smart, to allow certain selected customers to open accounts — though these were weekly accounts and had to be 'settled promptly'. Among those given this privilege were three who would hardly have been regarded as the most reliable members of society: Lillie Langtry, Ellen Terry and Oscar Wilde. But they were celebrities; as one writer has observed, 'their fame was their fortune, and they no doubt shed lustre upon the emporium.'

RIGHT: *Shortly after the new premises opened in 1884, a local newspaper, the Chelsea Herald, published an article extolling the quality of Harrod's Store and comparing it favourably with its grander West End rivals.*

For the staff, hours were long: from 7.30 a.m. to 9 p.m. on weekdays and to 11 p.m. on Saturdays. 'Hard going right up to closing time, 11 o'clock, put the shutters up, sweep up the shop, and the rest of the evening to yourself,' remarked one assistant dryly. To encourage punctuality, Charles Digby Harrod would remove the steps leading to the staff entrance, thus forcing latecomers to pass his glass-panelled office in the centre of the ground floor. He still exacted his penny-halfpenny fines. 'No humbugging! Get on with it!' was his constant admonition. His prejudice against female employees was finally overcome in 1885 with the reluctant appointment of Ida Annie Fowle as a clerk in the counting house.

The staff used to refer to him as 'old seedy (C.D.) cake', but he was held in some affection. Unlike William Whiteley, Harrod was never accused of exploiting his employees. Unusually for the period, they were paid overtime and always received a bonus of the then not inconsiderable sum of a sovereign for their annual holiday. He never had the slightest trouble recruiting staff.

HARROD'S STORES LIMITED

By the time his father died in 1885, Charles Digby Harrod had begun to worry about the future. Although still in his forties, he tired easily; one day he fainted in his office. Not even a move nearer the store could alleviate the pressure of business. His only son showed no interest in joining the business. Finally deciding that he must retire, Harrod discussed the matter with his old associate Edgar Cohen.

Cohen was delighted to help. He shrewdly recognized the immense potential of Harrod's business. In 1889 it was Cohen who suggested that the store be floated on the stock exchange, and Cohen who organized its conversion to a limited liability company and selected a board of directors, though he did not take a seat on the board himself until five years later. Characteristically, Harrod wanted to sell his business for cash. He remained deaf to Cohen's advice that he take payment in the form of £1 founders' shares: he was quite happy with a £120,000 cash deal. The shares went to others and the two hundred that he could have had for £1 each were to be worth £200,000 in a few years.

BELOW: *Example of a share certificate and dividend warrant issued by Harrod's Stores Limited in the early twentieth century. The flotation of the company in 1889 made possible the phenomenal expansion that took place in the following two decades.*
OPPOSITE: *From a street directory of 1895: Harrods expanded eastwards, acquiring the leases of the neighbouring shops.* INSET: *The frontage in 1898.*

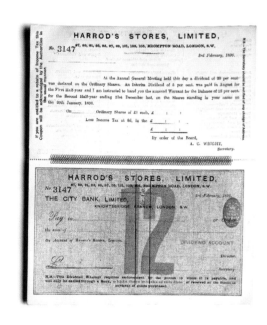

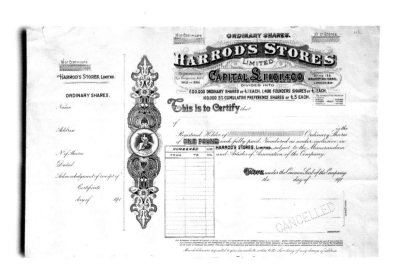

retail branch
61 Brown Edmund, tailor
63 Pike James, linendraper
65 Masters Edward, pawnbroker
67 to 77 *Gooch's Stores Lim.* outfitters
79 *Lockhart's Cocoa Rooms*
81 Moore Brothers Lim. tea mers
83 & 57 Randall H. E. Ltd. boot mas
85 *Singer Manufacturing Co. (The)*
85A, *District Messenger & Theatre Ticket Co. Lim. (The) (branch)*
..... *here is New street.* .....

87, 89, 91, 93, 95, 97, 99, 101, 103 & 105 *Harrods Limited*, grocers &c

107 & 109 De Coster Mrs. Mary, linendraper
..*here are Queen's gardens*..
111 *The Buttercup*, Henry Emanuel
113 Clarke Arthur James, hosier
115 Lilley & Skinner Lim. bootmas
117 & 123 Bridgland Richard J mantle maker
119 *United Kingd*
121 Cox W
123 &
125 B
131 Simons

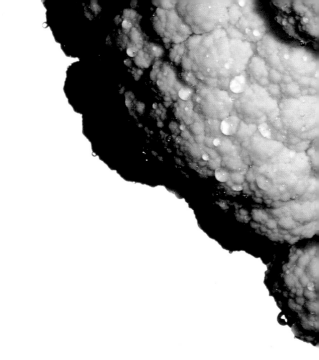

'Harrod's Stores Limited' came on the market in November 1889 for £141,400. In the year before going public, the takings had been estimated at £192,548; net profits for the preceding three years were £16,000 per annum.

Harrods was to remain a public company for the next ninety-five years, until, following its acquisition by Mohamed Al Fayed, it became once again a family business.

C.D. HARROD TO THE RESCUE

As part of his sale of the store, Charles Digby Harrod had stipulated that he was to have no more to do with its management. In the event, however, his retirement to Taunton in Somerset was short-lived. Hoping to maintain continuity, the board had appointed one of his chief assistants, William Smart, as manager — but things soon began to deteriorate. The worried directors, headed by the Chairman, Alfred Newton, begged Harrod to return temporarily. He agreed, and set about getting things back into order. The counting house worked overtime to sort out the chaotic bookkeeping.

Harrod repaired the damage so successfully that by Christmas 1890 the store could boast a profit of £12,479, enough to pay shareholders the promised 8 per cent dividend.

But Harrod's return could only be a stop-gap measure. The near-failure of the store had shown how much the success of the business had depended on the man at the helm. Once an able manager — Richard Burbidge — had been found for the store, Harrod retired for a second time. He lived for a further fifteen years, first in Somerset, then in Sussex and died aged sixty-four in 1905.

Honest, industrious, far-sighted, imbued with a spirit of service, Charles Digby Harrod had converted his father's modest grocery shop into a flourishing department store. By the end of his twenty-eight years in charge, the annual turnover was close to half-a-million pounds. It was no mean achievement.

As one of his old customers recalled:
'The first time I saw Charles Harrod he
expatiated to me on the beauty of his cauliflowers
and cabbages, in his stall shop front ...
... the last time I saw him was in a box
at the opera in immaculate garments and
beautiful gloves.'

Fortunately, Harrod's successor,
Richard Burbidge, was an exceptional man.
If the Harrods, father and son, had founded a
legend, then Burbidge was to raise the status of
their store to that of an international institution.

PALACE

OF

COMMERCE

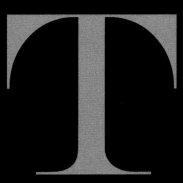

Harrods brings the Orient to Knightsbridge: one of the lavish catalogues issued in the Edwardian era. The artist has omitted the surrounding streets from his view of the store, so the palatial domed building appears to stand alone.

he story of Harrods is the story of a number of remarkable personalities. Some telling similarities are apparent. The description of Charles Digby Harrod as a demanding but fair employer is equally applicable to Richard Burbidge and, in more recent times, to Mohamed Al Fayed. The outstanding characteristic of all three is a combination of vision, energy and dedication. Unflinching in their resolve, they may have driven others hard but they were always prepared to drive themselves harder.

The particular contribution of Charles Digby Harrod was to see the potential for his father's shop and to realize that potential. The contribution of Richard Burbidge was to see the potential of the island site on which Harrods stands, and to display the tenacity and negotiating skills to acquire and develop it.

Mohamed Al Fayed's contribution has been to visualize what Harrods should be at a time when retailing has been going through fundamental changes, to create a palace of commerce and a place of fantasy that is nevertheless true to its heritage and history. He has shown the resolve and boldness to drive through this vision against a background of often unfavourable trading conditions.

That these men were right in their convictions is obvious in hindsight; so obvious that it is easy to forget how imaginative their ideas were when they were conceived.

RICHARD BURBIDGE

By the time Richard Burbidge was appointed General Manager of Harrods at the age of forty-four in 1891, he already had a formidable reputation, but few could have foreseen the scale of the transformation he was to bring about.

Born in 1847, the fourth of nine sons of a Wiltshire farmer, young Burbidge had come to London in 1862, to be apprenticed to a fellow Wiltshireman, Jonathan Puckeridge, a provisions, grocery and wine merchant in Oxford Street. Then, for fourteen years, he had run his own little grocery shop, Burbidge Brothers, in Upper George Street off the Edgware Road. In 1881 he had decided to sell the business and go into management, first at the Army & Navy Stores and then at Whiteleys in Westbourne Grove, which at that time was the largest department store in London. Burbidge remained at Whiteleys as General Manager for almost nine years, before leaving to manage a new venture called the Kensington Stores.

It was from here that he was lured away to Harrod's Stores, after much coaxing by Edgar Cohen and Alfred Newton. They could not have made a better choice. Burbidge knew all there was to know about department stores, and had proved his exceptional skills as a manager and organizer. Moreover, he had learned from William Whiteley, the 'Universal Provider', how to think big and get noticed.

ABOVE: *Richard Burbidge with his wife, Emily, in 1868, by which time Burbidge was running his own little grocery shop in Marylebone.*
BELOW: *On Burbidge's arrival at Harrods as General Manager in 1891, the expansion of the store began in earnest, as the leases to the adjoining shops were acquired. (Photograph c. 1892).*

Richard Burbidge was a rigidly self-disciplined man; he neither smoked nor drank, and he was up at five most mornings. To transform Charles Digby Harrod's relatively modest store into a world-famous institution, Burbidge needed to be what he was: ambitious, innovative, adventurous and, above all, industrious. No one without a vein of ruthlessness could have matched his achievements. Yet he was a kindly and sympathetic man, genuinely concerned with the welfare of his workforce and personally committed to public service and charitable works.

BURBIDGE THE BUILDER

Knightsbridge, at the time that Richard Burbidge took over as General Manager of Harrod's Stores in 1891, was changing rapidly. It was a district of contrasts. There were still appalling slums, yet just two or three streets away were the smart, new houses of Pont Street and Hans Place; tall, cliff-like blocks of luxury flats, in red brick with stone dressings, were already beginning to appear. From these, Harrod's Stores was to draw many of its customers.

Like his later successor Mohamed Al Fayed, Richard Burbidge was a great builder. It is to him that we owe the creation of a building which not only replaced the slums but which set the tone for this newly-fashionable area. Burbidge had always enjoyed a little property speculation, even when he was a humble grocer; now he was given the chance to play a major part in the redevelopment of the district.

In 1891 Harrod's Stores occupied about one-sixteenth of a large
block bounded by Brompton Road in the north, New Street (now
Hans Crescent) in the east, Hans Road in the west and Upper
North Street in the south. Much of the rest of the site was filled
with a huddle of poor housing and little yards, as George Weston,
who joined the staff in the last years of Charles Digby Harrod's
time, remembered:

> *I have never seen so much poverty as existed in the neighbourhood.*
> *There was a street called North Street, where people were herded together like*
> *so many animals... There was a narrow passage, very dark, that led into Queen's*
> *Gardens; these gardens contained little cottages at the back of which there was*
> *a large wood yard...*

Today Knightsbridge is one of the most prestigious
areas of London. The development of Harrods played no small
part in this remarkable transformation.

Burbidge's ambition was for Harrod's Stores
to occupy the entire island site. With boundless energy and iron
resolve he set about realizing his dream. It proved an epic
battle. By the end of 1893 he had bought out all but one
of the shops running along the Brompton Road frontage,
from New Street to the passage — about halfway along
today's frontage. But the owner of the draper's shop on the
corner, Cornelius de Coster, resolutely refused to relinquish his
lease. Not until after his death, in 1900, was his widow persuaded
to part with it.

A TERRACOTTA LANDMARK

In the meantime Burbidge turned his attention to the south side
of the site. In November 1894 the London County Council
decided to clear the slums bordering Upper North Street.
In doing so, they got rid of Upper North Street altogether and
created a new, parallel road, to be called Basil Street.
(New Street, in the east, was renamed Hans Crescent.)
Burbidge immediately put in a bid for the cleared land.
He was successful. This allowed him to extend the store as far
back as the new Basil Street. The architect for this new
extension was the now little-known C.W. Stephens, who had
already built some of the new houses in the area and
whose other work included Claridges in Mayfair and the nearby
store, Harvey Nichols. Harrods was to be Stephens's masterpiece.

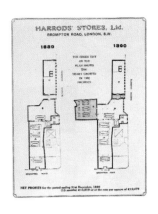

*Some of the plans
in series published
by Harrods in a
1910 brochure,
charting the growth
of the premises
over the previous
twenty-one years.
The expansion
accomplished in
each year was
marked in green.*
OPPOSITE:
*Swags and flowers
on the ornate
Edwardian
terracotta frontage.*

It was on this extension that the familiar Harrods terracotta appeared for the first time. Terracotta, much of it produced by the famous Doulton factory, was a popular building material in the late Victorian period. It was characteristic of the district, having been used for the Royal Albert Hall and the South Kensington museums, but nowhere was it employed with such verve as at Harrods. It was an inspired choice of material: it gave the store its glowing colour, part-rose, part-caramel, which is one of its most distinctive features.

The three upper floors of the new buildings in Basil Street and Hans Crescent were built as luxury apartments; Burbidge believed that customers preferred to shop on or near ground level. Besides, the apartments provided the store with a valuable source of income for many years.

In 1895 Burbidge was able to buy the head lease of all the properties on Brompton Road, westwards from the passage to Hans Road, with the exception of the pub on the corner, 'The Buttercup'. The owner was holding out for a better price. In fact two pubs — 'The Buttercup' and 'The Friend at Hand' — caused Burbidge the most trouble. In 1902 the owner of 'The Buttercup' finally capitulated and sold his lease for £25,000. But 'The Friend at Hand' held out until 1910, and for a time it even had to be incorporated into the store. A year later, in 1911, Burbidge finally gained control of the few remaining properties in Hans Road. Within twenty years of taking over Harrods, Burbidge had secured the entire four-and-a-half acre site.

EDWARDIAN OPULENCE

By 1902, after the eventual yielding of Mrs de Coster and 'The Buttercup', Richard Burbidge was in full possession of the Brompton Road frontage. This enabled him to put in hand his plans for rebuilding. He wanted to create an edifice which would outshine, not only Whiteleys, but any other department store.

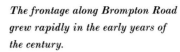

The frontage along Brompton Road grew rapidly in the early years of the century.
BOTTOM LEFT: *1901, the shop built by Charles Digby Harrod in 1884 is overshadowed by the first section of the great terracotta building of today.*
BELOW AND RIGHT: *1902-1904, the old shop is swept away, together with 'The Buttercup' public house, and de Coster's drapery shop. The lower two floors of the new building were made ready for trading before the construction of the flats on the floor above.*
TOP RIGHT: *1905, the frontage is complete with its grand central dome and the cupola on the turret at the corner of Hans Road.*

The latest steel-frame construction techniques were used and work progressed at breathtaking speed. Again Stephens was the architect. To enable trading to continue with minimum inconvenience to the customers, construction was in sections. In all, the project took four years to complete, from August 1901 to June 1905. The final section, on the extreme right-hand corner as one faces the building, was completed in the record time of six weeks; this included the demolition of an existing building and the erection of a seven-storey, turreted and elaborately detailed replacement.

Again the upper floors were given over to flats and called 'Hans Mansions'; the magnificent entrance portal to these apartments can still be seen in Hans Road.

Few buildings in London capture, so comprehensively, the exuberant spirit of the Edwardian age. Everything – its great dome, its embellished pediment with Britannia receiving the produce of the world, its rich detailing, its pillars and urns and balustrades – seems to encapsulate this high summer of the British Empire. Yet the building was not pompous. There was a lightness, an almost Parisian look to it. The huge, plate-glass windows were surmounted by delicate art nouveau tracery; the facade was enlivened with sculptured fruit and flowers, swags and cherubs. The style has been described as 'an eclectic amalgam of Second Empire and Baroque'. The effect was as much Belle Époque as Imperial Apogee.

HARRODS 1909

Departments for hardware, furniture and toys occupied the first floor at this end of the building; the more luxurious fashion departments were at the far end.

The baroque dome was built for show; it contained nothing more than a water tank.

Until the mid-1920s the grocery and provision departments were situated at the front of the building; like other ground-floor departments, they had lightwells to the floor above.

The fragrances of the perfumery department greeted customers entering from Brompton Road

One of the lifts linking the ground floor with the first-floor departments.

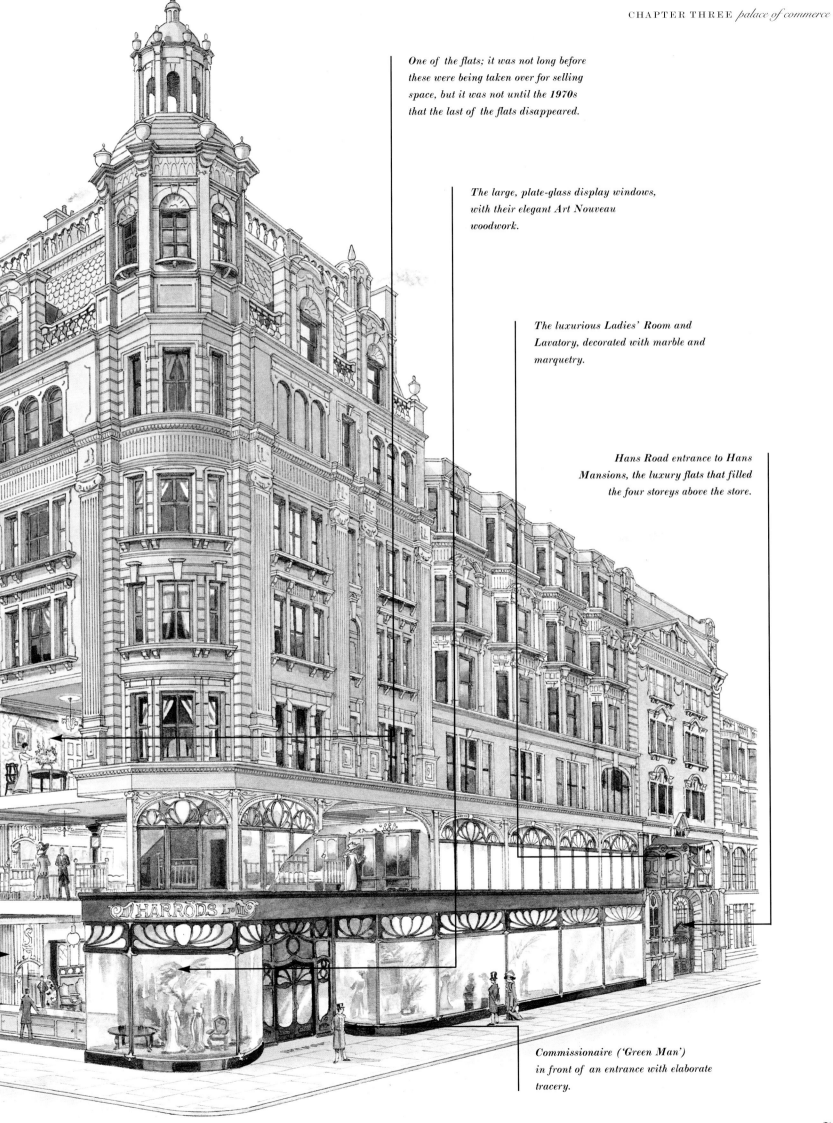

One of the flats; it was not long before these were being taken over for selling space, but it was not until the 1970s that the last of the flats disappeared.

The large, plate-glass display windows, with their elegant Art Nouveau woodwork.

The luxurious Ladies' Room and Lavatory, decorated with marble and marquetry.

Hans Road entrance to Hans Mansions, the luxury flats that filled the four storeys above the store.

Commissionaire ('Green Man') in front of an entrance with elaborate tracery.

The interior of the store, too, was transformed; it soon surpassed anything that had been previously attempted in shopfitting. The decoration and fittings were entrusted to the firm of Frederick Sage, Limited. Indeed, the work on Harrods occupied Sage's entire staff for the first five years of the century.

Connected by archways lined with mirrors, each department was decorated in a different but equally opulent style. Plasterers were brought from Paris to create the magnificent ceilings: extravagant plasterwork garlands in the Floral Hall and delicate Louis Quinze Rococo in the departments devoted to Ladies' Fashions. There were 'richly carved fittings in Ancona walnut' in the Millinery Department; polished satinwood fittings 'in the Egyptian style with introductions of superb marqueterie panelling' in the Ladies' Hairdressing Salon; chairs upholstered in green corded silk, Indian carpets on parquet floors, stained-glass windows, marble walls and onyx panels in the Ladies' Club. The Dining Rooms were decorated in what was described as 'the François Premier style'. The banking hall, called the Royal Exchange, was a riot of coloured marbles, fluted columns and mahogany counters with elaborate wrought-iron grilles.

In 1906 an American visitor, Joseph Appel of Wanamakers, at first thought the decoration was 'overdone'. But he soon changed his mind. 'Mr Burbidge says they get the

The 1904 general catalogue was illustrated with views of the new departments.
CLOCKWISE FROM TOP LEFT:
Hardware; Perfumery with view through to the Toy department above; the Grill Room, the store's first restaurant; the Floral Hall; Provisions; Pianos; Grocery.

land so cheap… that they can afford to spend money on luxurious fittings. But really it is because they are among such elaborate surroundings in London, beautiful public buildings, elaborate castles and private homes and so on, that they have to decorate more luxuriously than we do.' Appel was impressed by the quantity of carved mahogany and walnut, and the lavish use of marble. He also liked the carpets 'especially woven for them, sort of red with a figure' on the ground floor, while on the first floor they were 'lighter and more delicate, a sort of salmon pink'.

Most spectacular of all was the Meat Hall. Crowned by a high, elaborately ornamented skylight, it was lined with Doulton tiles to the designs of W. J. Neatby. In the upper level are Neatby's exquisite roundels, with their hunting scenes and goose girls, while below are his stylized wall decorations, which refer to the produce sold in the hall. Remarkably, the whole ensemble was devised and put together in a mere nine weeks. The hall attracted considerable interest both at home and abroad when it was unveiled in 1903; the journal of the Museum of Applied Arts in Vienna praised it as 'a triumph of original modern style and practical application of sound principles'. It remains one of Harrods' greatest treasures, and its recent restoration has brought out the richness and splendour of its colours.

BELOW: *Harrods Meat Hall put on impressive Christmas displays. The staff were photographed for posterity with this array of turkeys in 1922.*

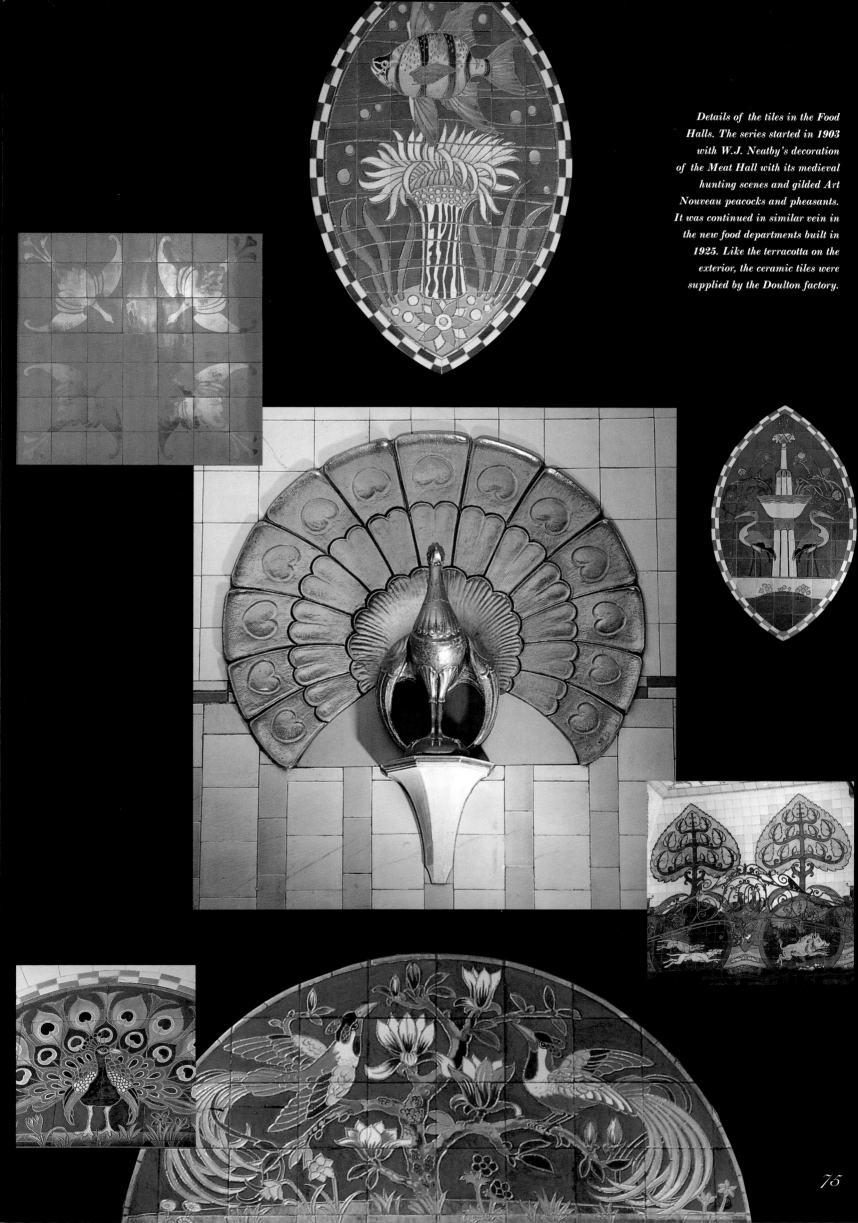

Details of the tiles in the Food Halls. The series started in 1903 with W.J. Neatby's decoration of the Meat Hall with its medieval hunting scenes and gilded Art Nouveau peacocks and pheasants. It was continued in similar vein in the new food departments built in 1925. Like the terracotta on the exterior, the ceramic tiles were supplied by the Doulton factory.

75

Butchers in the Meat Hall.
Built in 1903, this one of
the most splendid interiors
in London. Harrods Food
Halls are as famous for
their architectural delights
as they are for the quality
of their produce and the
expertise of their staff.

Underlying this magnificence was the very latest technology. As the Meat Hall required cold storage, Harrods engineers were obliged to devise a cooling system. Three artesian wells were bored, the deepest of which was almost 500 feet; sunk into the London chalk, they supply pure water to this day. Huge blocks of ice, made from this water, were placed at the bottom of air shafts during the summer to create a permanent supply of cool air. By 1908, electrical generators had been installed. For the following dozen or so years, Harrods was able to meet all its own electricity needs. Today, the store generates about 70 per cent of the electricity it consumes – enough to supply a small town.

Harrods' own supply of pure water, provided by three artesian wells dug deep beneath the London clay. The well water has been filtered through chalk since falling as rain on the uplands near London.

CLAY

WATER LEVEL

ROCK

The irrepressible Burbidge had planned yet another architectural feature: a 200-foot Coronation Tower. Like the new Georgian Restaurant on the fourth floor, this would commemorate the crowning of King George V in 1911 and, by coincidence, Harrods' acquisition of the last piece in the jigsaw of the island site. But it was never built. Nearby residents complained and the project was shelved. All that remains of Burbidge's grandiose scheme is a massive arch in Hans Road, and a foundation stone, laid by Richard Burbidge on 13 September 1911.

The Georgian Restaurant, an illustration from the 1914 general catalogue. The name commemorates the Coronation of King George V in 1911.

HARRODS' GEORGIAN RESTAURANT.

This magnificent Salon constitutes the largest Restaurant in London, having seating capacit
and Tea may be enjoyed in the most recherché style at moderate charges. A first-
The Restaurant is reached by lifts from the Furnishing Drapery Departmen

RENDEZVOUS OF FASHION AND LUXURY.

,000 guests at one time. It is noted for its dainty cuisine and excellent service. Luncheon
ring orchestra is a feature, and comfortable resting and retiring rooms are attached.
mmer the capacious out-door verandahs are much appreciated by visitors.

BEYOND BROMPTON ROAD

As the store expanded, storage space was as important as selling space. In 1893 Burbidge bought a disused soap factory at Barnes, the West London suburb where he had his home. It cost £16,200. This was to grow into a complex of buildings, including the famous Barnes Depository, in its time one of the largest warehouses in Europe. It was built as a depository where customers travelling overseas could store their furniture — a useful service in the days of the British Empire. Later, the space was used as warehouses for the store. However, since the opening in 1989 of the new Osterley Distribution Centre, the warehouses at Barnes have no longer been needed.

The handsome brick and terracotta building was much admired by Sir John Betjeman. In a 1971 BBC film about Harrods he contemplated the mass of deposited furniture. 'Floor after floor of uninhabited furnished rooms,' he mused. 'Uninhabited except by ghosts.'

Some of the goods came up by river. Indeed, the depository, with its prominently lettered 'Harrod's', invariably caused confusion during the annual Oxford vs Cambridge boat race. Radio listeners would be startled to hear that the boats were 'just passing Harrods'.

Burbidge's acquisition of property in Knightsbridge was not restricted to the island site. Yet more storage space — and space for dispatch, bakeries and workshops — was provided by acquiring a site across the Brompton Road, at the southern end of Trevor Square. To link the new building to the store, a tunnel had to be constructed under the Brompton Road. It became another in that bewildering warren of quaintly-named passageways that run under the store today. And there were other Harrods outposts nearby: in Draycott Avenue, Pentagon Place, Brompton Place, Pavilion Road, and Lancelot Place, where an old chapel was converted into an early showroom for bicycles and motor cars.

To realize his dreams of expansion Burbidge had to persuade his sometimes hesitant board of directors and convince doubting shareholders. But he knew what he was doing. The figures speak for themselves: annual profits had risen from £12,479 in 1891, the year that Burbidge took over, to £309,227 in 1913. By then the annual turnover was in the region of £4 million.

TOP: *A bottle of Harrods VOH Whisky, sent in a food parcel to the front in 1917. It came back unopened with its wounded recipient, who kept it as a lucky souvenir, and it is now in the Harrods Archive.*
ABOVE: *Elegant packaging: an embossed cardboard box from the 1900s. The Harrods emblem, a winged woman emptying a cornucopia over the world, first appeared in the 1890s.*
OPPOSITE: *Harrods Depository, by the Thames at Barnes, was built for customers to store their furniture. It was later used as warehousing.*

THE HARRODS KNOW-HOW

I t is the responsibility of the buyers to ensure that Harrods Food Halls are stocked with only the finest fresh produce and the only way to achieve this is by getting up before dawn each morning to go to market.

Though the opening bell at Billingsgate Fish Market is not rung until 5.00 a.m., the Harrods buyer will be there by 4.30 to select the finest catch from around the world. From Oman, the Seychelles, Portugal and France, come fish of all colours, shapes and sizes.

Once bought, the fish are immediately loaded into a refrigerated Harrods van for delivery to the store by 6.45 a.m.

All Harrods fish are displayed whole, not filleted, so that the customers can see for themselves that they are in good condition. The fishmongers will then fillet and prepare the chosen fish if required.

Every week, fish, meat and poultry is sent by the Food Halls to the restaurants, and cooked for formal blind-tasting sessions to ensure that it meets the store's high standards.

the perfect fish

Concern about healthy diet has made fish an increasingly popular dish, and the latest fashion is for exotic species like the parrot fish, pomfret and red admiral (photographed here).

Fresh fish have bright red gills, bright eyes and feel firm to the touch – what is known in the trade as 'stiff alive' – and any that do not meet these standards will be rejected.

April is the cheese buyer's favourite month, for it marks the beginning of the fresh goat's cheese season. And perhaps the most eagerly awaited cheeses are the little Banon – a succulent, melting chèvre wrapped in chestnut leaves – and the bûchette sarrette – a small log presented on a slat of wood and ripened with leaves of summer savory. Its clean, light, fresh taste is due to the fact that the goats which produced the milk, have grazed in fields of savory.

It is not only the taste that pleases, but the knowledge that these cheeses have been handmade by a sixty-year-old expert, who has adapted to modern standards, yet continues to make the most wonderful produce at his small farm in the lavender fields of Provence.

Each spring and autumn – the two main cheese seasons – the Harrods buyer visits Rungis, a town outside Paris that is entirely devoted to food. Since the closure of the Parisian markets at Les Halles, Rungis has become the centre of fine French foods.

Here there are six cheese halls and cellars stacked with row upon row of cheeses from which the buyer will taste and select the finest.

He also visits an *affineur*, or cheese ripener, near the Belgian border, who buys from artisan cheese-makers all over France. There is much tasting and discussion before a selection of cheeses is made. These are delivered to Harrods at various stages of ripening: some will be ready to eat and others will be ripened in the store's own cellar. Turning and wrapping the cheeses is a full-time job.

The market for traditional British cheeses has grown considerably in recent years. The buyer travels the length and breadth of the country supporting small, local producers. They include the Stilton dairy in Saxelbye, Leicestershire, which has been handed down through the same family since the end of the last century, and the Appleby family's Cheshire dairy – as well as eighty-year-old Mrs Kirkham, who is still making traditional Lancashire cheese, and Mary Holbrook near Bath, who specializes in Mediterranean-style cheeses.

There are over **300** cheeses on offer, from Spain, Italy, Corsica and Madeira, as well as from France and Britain, so all Harrods assistants are trained to help the customer make their selection. They will give slices to taste, recommend those cheeses which have reached maturity, provide recipes and suggest suitable wines or beers (often these will have been produced in the same region as the cheese).

the perfect cheese

BURBIDGE THE REFORMER

The staff at Harrods had viewed Burbidge's arrival with some trepidation. Whiteley had a reputation as a bad employer, and Burbidge had been Whiteley's right-hand man. They need not have worried: his experience at Whiteleys had taught Burbidge the importance of good staff relations. He immediately set about improving conditions. The long hours were reduced; the shop now closed at seven each evening, at eight on Fridays and at nine on Saturdays. He also introduced an early-closing day. He abolished Charles Digby Harrod's fines for lateness. He instituted cost price meals for the staff: bacon and eggs for breakfast, hot joints for lunch and cold meats for supper.

Among Burbidge's forward-looking reforms were a Provident Society and a Benevolent Fund, access to a medical officer and a dentist, and a Staff Council. Burbidge recognized the importance of staff training and education, at a time when the general level of public education was low. By 1914 he could claim to have introduced a scheme of 'yearly free scholarships, which provides for training in arithmetic, handwriting, commercial English, typewriting, French or Spanish, business efficiency and salesmanship, and special training on matters purely connected with the business of the house.' Burbidge even conducted Sunday Bible classes for the staff at his home.

The days when Ida Fowle had been the only woman employee had long since gone. As the store grew, new departments, such as drapery and ladies' fashions, led to the appointment of

Richard Burbidge knew that the health and motivation of his staff was vital for the success of the business. Shorter hours gave Harrodians more leisure to use the sporting and social facilities provided by the store. There were also evening classes. The Harrodian Club created a special sense of camaraderie.
ABOVE: *Water polo team, 1909.*
BELOW: *Rule book from 1936.*

HARRODIAN CLUB
WOMEN'S HOCKEY TEAM 1950 – 1951

T. BUGBY   S. OFFORD   V. HINES   M. CHANCE   R. YATES   W. BAKER   L. LAWS

B. BARNES   W. FROST   A. WALTON   E. LONG   S. STUART

HARRODIAN ROWING CLUB.   SEASON 1922.

many more female staff. Here too, Burbidge's reforming spirit was evident: a Ladies' Wednesday Evening Physical Culture Class was started, and during the First World War special courses were organized for women to learn business skills.

When he came to the store, Burbidge had kept on most of Charles Digby Harrod's staff (some, such as William Kibble, became trusted associates), but he also brought in former colleagues from Whiteleys. He was a good judge of character and knew to whom he could delegate, but he still kept a close eye on every detail of the running of the store. Every day, at 10 a.m. precisely, Burbidge with his four section managers (together with Burbidge's secretary) would set off on a tour of the entire store. Silk-hatted and frock-coated, the solemn procession would make its way through the store, inspecting, questioning, checking, and, now and then, stopping to chat to customers or junior assistants.

Burbidge's concern for his staff did not end with their working hours. In 1894 a piece of land near the Barnes Depository was set aside for the social and sporting use of his employees. Out of this developed the Harrodian Club and the Harrodian Amateur Athletic Association (all employees were expected to join). Staff were able to spend their longer leisure hours in rugby, soccer, hockey, rowing and running. In 1904 Burbidge bought Mill Lodge, a country house set in fourteen acres of land in Barnes, to provide a splendid setting for the Harrodian Club's activities and functions. All this helped strengthen a certain Harrods camaraderie, a specifically Harrodian identity.

When Richard Burbidge took over the store in 1891, the staff numbered 200; by the end of the century, it numbered over 2500; by the year of his death, 1917, Harrods employed 6000 people.

ABOVE: *Sir Woodman Burbidge with Harrodian oarsmen, 1922.*
TOP: *Women's hockey team, 1950-51.*

Illustrated booklets produced by the store, *The House That Every Woman Knows* (1909) and *The Wonderful Development of Harrods* (1910), showed the new departments peopled by exquisitely elegant customers. The Royal Exchange (ABOVE) was one of the grandest of the new interiors. The Ladies Club (RIGHT) gave weary shoppers a chance to rest.

'SOCIETY'S FAVOURITE STORE'

It was Burbidge who devised the store's first motto, *Omnia Omnibus Ubique*, and its first trademark: the image of a winged young woman, seated on a globe and pouring a rich variety of goods from a cornucopia of merchandise.

In the Edwardian golden age of department stores, when so many London shops were expanding, Burbidge had made Harrods pre-eminent. It had not only overtaken Whiteleys, it had also set the standards by which stores could be judged. Shopping, by the turn of the century, had changed dramatically. The public was now confronted by an unprecedented wealth of merchandise from all over the British Empire and the rest of the world. The spread of the railways, the convenience of omnibus travel, the increasing wealth of the middle classes, the gradual emancipation of women, all contributed

to a spectacular growth in shopping as a leisure pursuit. Harrods had been given a boost by the opening in 1906 of Knightsbridge Underground station, making the store easily accessible to many more shoppers.

Harrods could no longer claim to offer goods at the lowest prices, as it had in Charles Digby Harrod's time. Instead it could offer a luxurious shopping experience unrivalled in the metropolis, and an unparalleled range of goods and services.

By the end of the Edwardian period, Harrods had became known as the store for the rich and the well-born: 'Society's Favourite Store'. It was considered perfectly proper for a lady to meet a gentleman in one of its tea-rooms or restaurants. An illustrated booklet, *The House That Every Woman Knows*, produced to celebrate the store's Diamond Jubilee in 1909 depicts Harrods as a fashionable rendezvous. Top-hatted gentlemen in frock coats escort women with pouter-pigeon figures in outsize hats and feather boas through a series of sumptuously appointed departments.

HARRODS IN THE HEADLINES

Burbidge had a gift for publicity, especially if the publicity was in a good cause. Harrods' continuing association with charitable work dates from his time. In 1895, when the *Daily Telegraph*

GUIDE TO DEPARTMENTS ON GROUND FLOOR.

OVER 100 DEPARTMENTS UNDER ONE ROOF, FORMING THE MOST COMPLETE, LUXURIOUS AND UP-TO-DATE EMPORIUM IN THE WORLD.

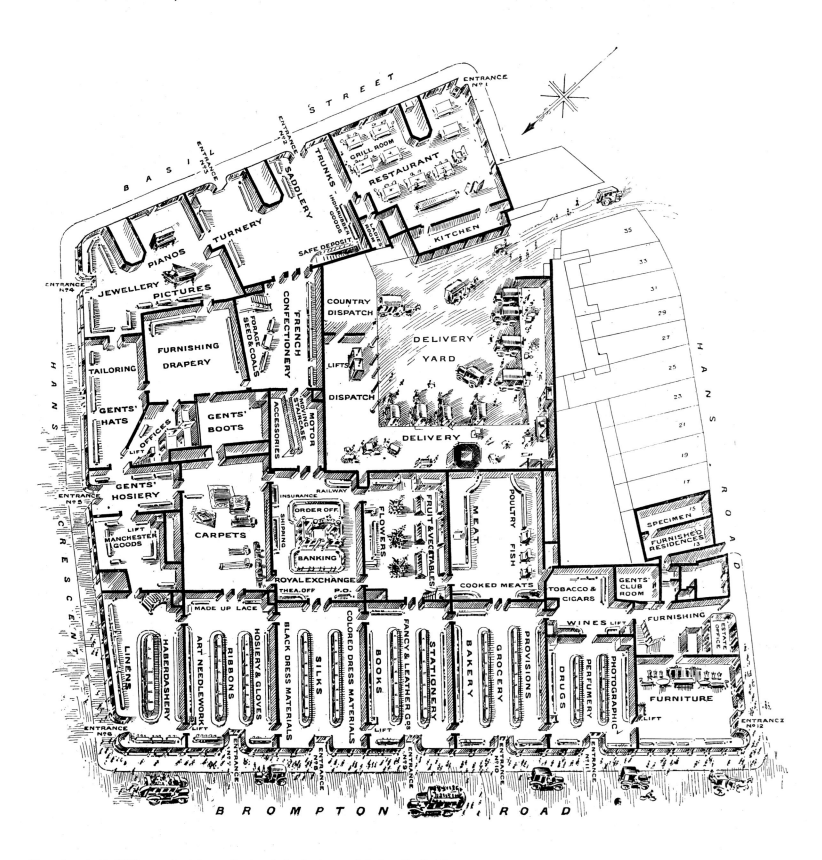

Floor plans in the 1909 general catalogue; the store had not yet expanded above the first floor.
The rest of the Hans Road site (on the right of the plans) was acquired the following year.

GUIDE TO DEPARTMENTS ON FIRST FLOOR.

TO BE REACHED BY NUMEROUS LIFTS AND MOVING STAIRWAY. THE SHOPPING AREA ALONE IS OVER 36 ACRES.

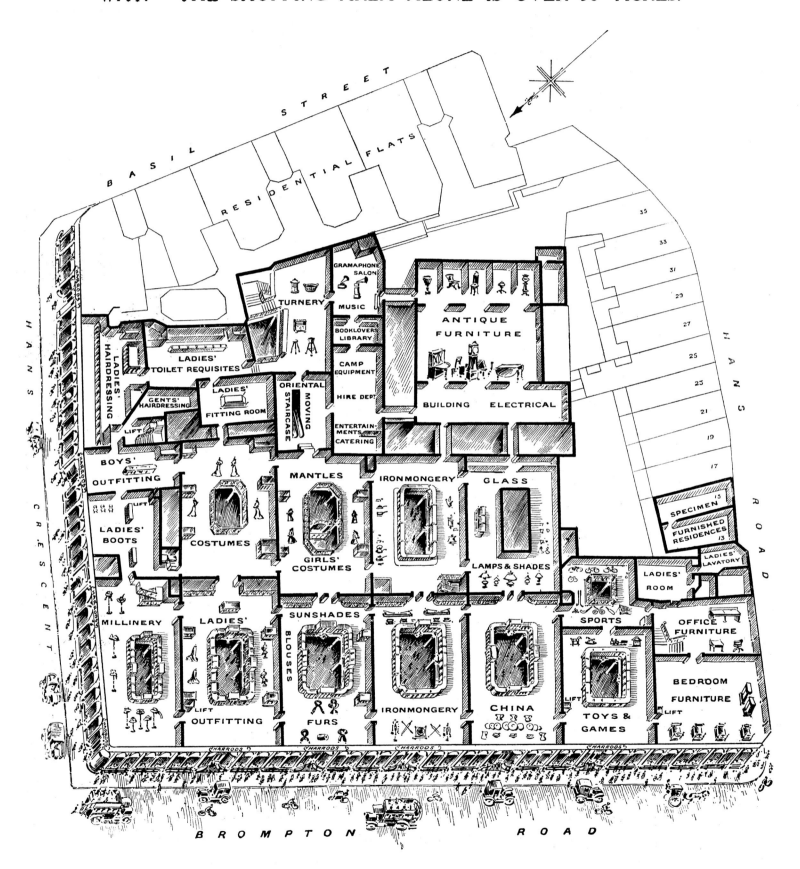

newspaper organized a collection in aid of 'Christmas Dinners for Cripples', it was Harrod's Stores that provided the hampers. On Christmas Eve the store's twenty-eight pantechnicon vans lined up at Barnes, each with 160 hampers inside. All were delivered on time. But Burbidge was capable of occasional misjudgements. On the occasion of Queen Victoria's Diamond Jubilee in 1897, for instance, the store built stands along the processional route. The seats were to be let to customers, who were also to be provided with luncheon. Unfortunately there were not enough takers, and Harrods suffered a considerable financial loss. But the store's directors never lost their confidence in Burbidge's abilities.

THE MOVING STAIRCASE

A stir could be created by novelties in the store. One of the most sensational appeared in 1898, when the first moving staircase in London was installed, with Harrods acquiring the British patent. It was not, strictly speaking, a moving staircase at all: merely a gently inclined conveyor belt that carried customers from the ground floor to the first floor. Press reaction was ecstatic, with much talk of 'magic carpets' and of being 'wafted by imperceptible motion'. In case any shoppers should be overcome by this heady experience, an attendant was on hand to administer cognac or sal volatile.

The publicity was a resounding success; Mrs Stuart Menzies, Burbidge's biographer, recalled:

...all the children in London and a good many in the country were making their parents' lives burdens to them, until they promised to take them to Harrod's Stores to go on their new moving staircase. I was taken there by a youngster of my own who insisted on going up and down this staircase. Then, of course, when once in the Stores it was well to do some shopping, and the young people wanted good things, and so forth. People thronged to see that moving staircase (electric); the carriage loads of children being unpacked at the door might have led to the belief that a Christmas pantomime was being performed in the Stores. Personally I thought the sensation of being carried upwards without any movement or exertion on my part was not altogether pleasant; but I never was a good sailor!

OPPOSITE: *The famous 'moving staircase' – in fact more of a conveyer belt – was a great publicity coup in 1898.* BELOW: *Customers eagerly sampled the exhilarating experience (photograph c. 1902). These pictures give a glimpse of the interior of the old building erected by Charles Digby Harrod, before it was rebuilt in 1903.*

HARRODS, Limited, Brompton Road, London, S.W.

THE "MOVING STAIRCASE,"

NOW RUNNING DAILY FOR THE CONVENIENCE OF CUSTOMERS.

PRESS QUOTATIONS.

"MORNING POST."

"A remarkable substitute for the ordinary lift or elevator, which is quite a novelty in this country. . . . . There need never be any of those vexatious waits which occur when an ordinary lift is in use."

"SKETCH."

"By a delightful movement which is both exhilarating and fascinating, you are carried from floor to floor without the least effort, and without any of those unpleasant thrills which lifts always succeed in giving to nervous persons. . . . . I think they will find it so popular that there will scarcely be a Store or a great trading business in London that will not be glad to institute the same invention."

"WAREHOUSEMAN AND DRAPE

"There can be no doubt the usefulness of the inven and they should soon be in ge use in railway stations, pu buildings, hotels, warehou &c."

Not every innovation was an unqualified success. The new 'dry shampoo' treatment was much in vogue at the beginning of the century, until disaster struck in Harrods hairdressing salon in 1909. When the volatile mixture (94 per cent carbon tetrachloride, 1.5 per cent carbon disulphide and 4.5 per cent perfumed water) was used on the head of Miss Helenora Catharine Elphinstone-Dalrymple, she collapsed. The distraught shampooist, Beatrice Clark, then did the worst possible thing: she laid her unconscious client on the floor, which simply allowed the shampoo vapour to affect Miss Elphinstone-Dalrymple even more lethally.

It emerged at the inquest that the young lady already had a serious heart condition, and Beatrice Clark and her superior were exonerated — but the potential dangers of 'dry shampoo' had been revealed. Never again did Harrods shampoo a customer to death.

Gentlemen's Hairdressing, photographed c. 1907, was equipped with the latest trichological technology. (Note the motor-driven rotating brushes for buffing bald pates.) In 1930 it was replaced by the American-style, art deco barber-shop installed below the new Man's Shop.

The Ladies' Hairdressing Salon in 1919. Furnished in the Empire style – its individual cubicles glazed with engraved and frosted glass – it was grander and more extensive than its masculine counterpart.
BELOW RIGHT: *Gordon Selfridge, late of Marshall Field in Chicago, opened his Oxford Street store to a fanfare of publicity in 1909, but Harrods' counterblast was effective.*

An altogether more successful innovation was the introduction of the first pneumatic tube system for inter-departmental communication. This was installed after Richard Burbidge's trip to the United States in 1904, during which he visited the famous Macys in New York. The tour considerably increased his enthusiasm for expansion, Here was a store with nine floors, five escalators and no less than thirty-three lifts. It also weakened his conviction that customers would never shop on higher levels.

An indication of the standing of Richard Burbidge by this time, is the fact that, when visiting Washington, he was shown over the White House by President Theodore Roosevelt himself. Burbidge remained friendly with the owners of Macys, the Straus family. The Harrods archives contain a copy of a poignant letter from Isidor and Ida Straus, posted from Le Havre, just before they set sail on the maiden voyage of the *Titanic*. They had dined with the Burbidges the previous evening.

A NEW RIVAL

Only in 1909, when the ebullient American businessman, Gordon Selfridge, arrived in London and erected his eight-storey, purpose-built, undeniably imposing store in Oxford Street, did Harrods' self-confidence waver. But not for long. By a happy coincidence, March 1909 — the date on which Selfridges was to open — was also the sixtieth anniversary, the Diamond Jubilee, of the founding of Harrods. Or so it was claimed.

A 'Commemoration Week' was launched. The store was 'converted into a huge bower of natural flowers', there was a special spring fashion show, the London Symphony Orchestra was hired to perform, and no less a personality than Richard Haldane, Secretary of State for War, was invited to make the opening address. (In the event, press criticism of cabinet ministers giving publicity to department stores persuaded Haldane to withdraw his acceptance.)

To counter Selfridge's boast of paying the best rates in London, each member of staff at Harrods was given an extra week's wages.

GAIETY THEATRE

MANAGING DIRECTOR — Mr. GEORGE EDWARDES.

Every Evening at 8, MATINEE every Saturday at 4
Mr. GEORGE EDWARDES' New Production,

"OUR MISS GIBBS,"

A Musical Play by "CRYPTOS."
Constructed by JAMES T. TANNER.
Music by IVAN CARYLL.
Lyrics by ADRIAN ROSS and PERCY GREENBANK
and LIONEL MONCKTON.

The Honourable Hughie Pierrepoint (an Amateur
Criminal) Mr. GEORGE GROSSMITH, Jun.
The Earl of St. Ives ... (Lord Eynsford's Father)
Mr. O. H. CLARENCE
Slithers ...(a Professional Crook) ... Mr. ROBERT HALE
Mr. Toplady ... (Manager at Garrod's)
Mr. ARTHUR HATHERTON
Lord Eynsford ... (in love with Mary)
Mr. J. EDWARD FRASER
Mr. Beavis ... (the Earl's Family Solicitor)
Mr. J. A. BVELYN
A Taxi Cabby ... Mr. F. PAYNE
Mr. Amalfy ... (the Director General of
the White City) ... Mr. H. B. BURCHER
AND
Timothy Gibbs ... (Mary's Yorkshire Cousin)
Mr. EDMUND PAYNE

Lady Elizabeth Thanet ... (engaged to Lord
Eynsford) ... Miss DENISE ORME
Madame Jeanne ... (Modiste at Garrod's)
Miss JEAN AYLWIN
The Duchess of Minster ...(Lady Elizabeth's
Mother) Miss GLADYS HOMFREY
Mrs. Farquhar ... (an Impecunious Woman
of Fashion) Miss MAISIE GAY
Clarita ... Miss KITTY MASON
Nora ... (Colleens of Irish ... Miss OLIVE MAY
Sheilah ... { Village at the ... Miss ADELINE BALFE
Kathleen ... (White City) ... Miss ROSIE BEGARNIE
Lady Connie ... Miss GLADYS COOPER
Lady Sybil ... Miss JULIA JAMES
Lady Trixie ... Miss ENID LESLIE
Lady Angela ... Miss CHRISSY BELL
Lady Muriel ... Miss SUZANNE SELBOURNE
Lady Gwen ... Miss GERTIE THORNTON
AND
Mary Gibbs ("Our Miss Gibbs") Miss GERTIE MILLAR

Girls at the Stores:—Mesdames Madge Melbourne, Ida Barnard, Rhona Dalvy, Joe Howard, Gladys Carrington,
Pattie Wells, Irene Warren, Shirley Foster, Pauline Francis, Nancy More, Marjorie Michie, Marjorie Napier,
Ruby Kennedy, Ruth Argent, Gertrude Hirch, Marie Dean.
Dudes:—Messrs. G. Grundy, B. Camp, A. Fraser, J. Redmond, C. Cameron, S. Lyndon.

ACT I. ... ... Garrod's Stores (Joseph Harker.)
ACT II. ... Court of Honour at Franco-British Exhibition (Joseph Harker.)

The Play produced by Mr. GEORGE EDWARDES and Mr. EDWARD ROYCE.
Orchestra under the direction of Mr. IVAN CARYLL.
Costumes designed by SIGNOR COMELLI.

and executed by MARGAINE LACROIX, Paris, Madame LUCILE, Madame HAYES, Miss FISHER, B. J. SIMMONS & Co.,
Covent Garden, JOHNS & BONHAM, Ltd., 14 King Street, St. James; DURNINSHAW & ENSIGHTS, MORRIS ANGEL & SON.
Dresses in Act I. by Messrs. HARROD'S, Ltd.
Millinery by MAISON LEWIS, L. & L. LEVILLON, GAINSBOROUGH, Ltd., and Messrs. HARROD'S, Ltd.
Wigs by W. CLARKSON. Shoes by H. & M. RAYNE.
Properties by H. W. ELLIOTT. Furniture by J. S. LYON.
Electrical Effects by G. A. APPLEBEE. Machinist, J. SHELDON.

Stage Manager, Mr. EDWARD ROYCE.

BOX OFFICE (F. H. JUBB) OPEN DAILY, from 10 till 10.

The Bars in this Theatre are under the direct control of the Management, and all articles sold are specially
selected and guaranteed to be of the finest quality.

G. Hammersworth & Co., Printers, 18, Drury Lane, W.C.—Telephone 69, Central.

7460 A ROTARY PHOTO, E.C.
MR ARTHUR HATHERTON | MISS GERTIE MILLAR | "OUR MISS GIBBS." | MISS MAISIE GAY
AS "MR TOPLADY" | AS "MARY GIBBS" | | AS "MRS. FARQUHAR"

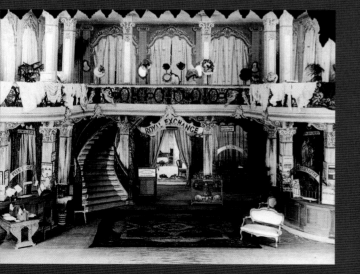

7460 B ROTARY PHOTO, E.C. | "OUR MISS GIBBS." | MISS GLADYS HOMFREY
MISS RUTH ARGENT | | AS "DUCHESS OF MINSTER"
AS "MME JEANNE" | | AS "LADY ..."

Chorus: Garrod's! Garrod's
If you are lacking
Whiting or blacking,
Lace or sacking:
Garrod's! Garrod's!
all things are there!
Brooches,
Coaches,
Tresses of hair,
Rosies,
Cosies,
Silk underwear –
Ev'rything for ev'rybody –
Ev'rywhere!

OPENING CHORUS

Lady Clients at Garrod's Stores

By Special Appoint-ment   to Her Majesty the Queen.

Harrods

The Fashion for Frills is well shown by the Charming Model Wrap here illustrated. It is one of many of the New Season's Styles to be seen just now in Harrods' Mantle Salons. Nowhere else can such a pleasing array be found in Coats and Wraps for Summer Wear at such attractively moderate prices.

"Longchamps"

A Chic Wrap for Summer, in bright soft chiffon taffeta. Stocked in Navy or Black. Price

6½ Gns.

To order in any colour, **10/6** extra.

Harrods Ltd. London S.W.

RICHARD BURBIDGE,
Managing Director.

HARRODS IN WARTIME

The tradition of public service which Richard Burbidge had established became evident when the country was at war. During the Boer War, which started in 1899, the store played its part. A public appeal by Sir Alfred Newton, the Chairman, and Lord Mayor of London in 1900, led to the rapid raising and equipping of the City Imperial Volunteers for service in South Africa. Much of this equipping was done by Harrods. The store even sent 1250 packed lunches to Southampton to welcome the men home.

The First World War saw an even greater involvement on the part of the store. The Building Department was kept busy constructing hospitals and other necessary buildings. The store's contract with the Belgian government eventually included the setting up and supplying of hospitals, laundries and aeroplane hangars. The catering services were also in demand; Harrods spent several months trying to obtain payment from a Canadian Army unit, whose officers' mess the store had provisioned when it was camped on Salisbury Plain.

It was, of course, impossible for Harrods to maintain its pre-war level of stock and services during the war years. The store laid on special exhibitions to promote the war effort, and advertised its own war bonds to help raise money. The catalogues reflect the spirit of the time; there are suggestions for gifts to send to men at the front, as well as uniforms for nurses and clothes suitable for women working on the land. Towards the end of the war, as food shortages began to bite, the store was offering such novel items as wedding cakes with sugar-free icing. 3200 staff members joined the forces; the names of the 147 who gave their lives are recorded on the memorial on No. 3 Staircase. They are commemorated, with those who fell in the Second World War, at a ceremony each Remembrance Day.

OPPOSITE: 'Fashion for Frills', an advertisement from April 1915, but Harrods was already directing its energies to the war effort.
BELOW: The impact of the First World War can be seen in these pages from 1917 issues of Harrods News, the catalogue sent weekly to customers.

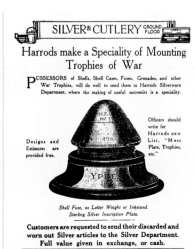

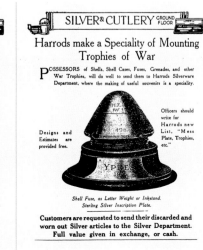

ROYALTY

Harrods' long association with the British royal family dates back to Burbidge's time. Queen Alexandra took an early interest in the store, and in 1910 Harrods was awarded its first royal warrant from Queen Maud of Norway (the daughter of King Edward VII), who was supplied by its furnishing and drapery departments.

The first official connection with the reigning King and Queen came in 1913 with a visit to the store by Queen Mary, accompanied by her only daughter Princess Mary. This was to inspect a special china and pottery exhibition. Escorted by the Chairman, Sir Alfred Newton, and Richard Burbidge, Queen Mary showed 'a wonderful practical knowledge' of the display. She not only 'appreciated the commercial advantage likely to result from the exhibition of British goods of such beauty in the heart of a wealthy and cultured community like that served by Harrods' but actually bought a few items herself.

After this first visit, Queen Mary was a frequent visitor to the store, her last visit being in 1951, two years before her death. Members of the staff remembered how, if early, she would insist on her chauffeur driving round the block as often as was necessary in order to arrive exactly on time for her welcome by the gratified Managing Director.

Queen Mary's 1913 visit resulted in the granting to Harrods of a special warrant of appointment as drapers and furnishers to Her Majesty, the first warrant from the British royal family. It was followed not long afterwards by a warrant from Queen Alexandra.

Today the store is one of the few to hold all four royal warrants: Harrods are suppliers of provisions and household goods to Queen Elizabeth II; suppliers of china, glass and fancy goods to Queen Elizabeth the Queen Mother; outfitters and saddlers to the Prince of Wales; and outfitters to the Duke of Edinburgh.

Not only British Royals shop at Harrods. The array of Royal Warrants on this letterhead from the 1930s includes the coats of arms of the reigning houses of Italy, Norway and Belgium.

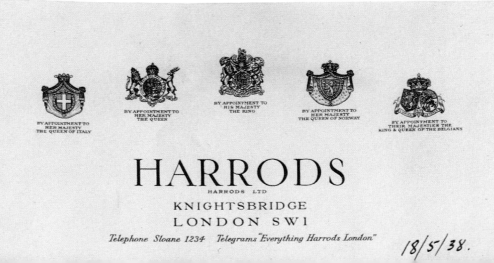

Harrods crossed the Atlantic in 1913, when it opened a store in Argentina. Harrods (Buenos Aires) is reminiscent of its 'mother' house, though the bright sunlight in this photograph suggests a different climate from Knightsbridge. It remained part of the Harrods Group until the 1960s.

'FATHER MADE HARRODS'

Richard Burbidge was a family man and was always proud of his Wiltshire origins. In 1868, at the age of twenty-one, he had married a local Wiltshire girl, Emily Woodman of Melksham. The couple had two sons and four daughters. In 1903 Burbidge bought himself a country property, Littleton Park near Shepperton, just outside London, which he set about extending and rebuilding. He and his family also had one of the new flats above the store. When the Brompton Road frontage was complete, they moved to 51 Hans Mansions at the front of the building.

His eldest son, Woodman Burbidge, had joined the company in 1893 as a junior query clerk, at £3 a week. He soon proved himself: his rapid promotion had less to do with the fact that he was the Managing Director's son than with his redoubtable business abilities. During his two visits to the United States and one to Canada, Richard Burbidge felt that he could safely leave Woodman in charge of the store.

In 1913 Woodman Burbidge travelled to Argentina to inaugurate his father's latest venture: Harrods in Buenos Aires. In his urge to expand the business, Burbidge had not only established a national institution, he was founding an international group. Harrods (Buenos Aires) Ltd was floated as a public company. Today the store in Buenos Aires has no links whatsoever with Harrods of Knightsbridge, and for many years there has been no connection between the companies.

In the New Year's Honours List of 1916, Richard Burbidge was rewarded with a baronetcy — chiefly for his charitable work. The honour was celebrated with a concert in the Albert Hall, which was filled with members of Harrods staff together with their families and friends. In March the following year, Burbidge turned seventy. But the pressures of his life — the relentlessness with which he had always driven himself — had taken their toll. Within two months, by the end of May 1917, he was dead.

Richard Burbidge's achievements — the creation of one of the most impressive buildings in London, and the transformation of a small store into the largest department store in Europe — had been remarkable. His eldest son, now Sir Woodman Burbidge, could hardly have given him a more fitting epitaph. 'Father', he said simply, 'made Harrods.'

In 1919 Harrods commissioned the photographer Bedford Lemere to take views of the various departments. His superbly composed photographs, with their eerily arranged shop dummies, are an invaluable record. The Ladies' Outfitting department in 1919: much of this fine rococo plasterwork dating from 1902 still survives.

WHITE PETTICOATS

Departments on the first floor, photographed by Bedford Lemere in 1919. CLOCKWISE FROM TOP LEFT: *Blouses; Toys; Corsets; and Ladies' Costumes. Lemere's photographs are empty of staff or customers, since they were taken out of opening hours.*

CHAPTER 4

THE BURBIDGE DYNASTY

Three generations of Burbidges.
FROM TOP LEFT:
The first Sir Richard Burbidge (1847-1917), Sir Woodman Burbidge (1872-1945), and the second Sir Richard Burbidge (1897-1966).

ichard Burbidge had not only, in his son's words, 'made' Harrods, he had also founded a dynasty. He was succeeded as Managing Director by his son Woodman Burbidge who, in turn, was succeeded by his son, the second Richard. So for almost seventy years — from 1891 until 1959 — the effective control of Harrods was in the hands of one family.

Forty-five when he took over in 1917, Sir Woodman Burbidge was a very different man from his father and he faced a very different set of problems. Woodman was not a visionary;

107

he was above all an astute merchant, a planner and an administrator. He certainly needed all his administrative skills during the difficult years following the end of the First World War. Harrods had to adjust to the new post-war conditions. The old, hierarchical Edwardian world was giving way to a more egalitarian social order. The atmosphere at Harrods, complained one employee, was 'too snobbish and unctuous'. He protested that the post-war Harrodian 'is a different type of chap from his Victorian prototype.'

These changes had to be reflected in the running of the store. Sir Woodman could not have hoped to continue along the autocratic lines of his father's day. One of his first moves was to reduce the power of the buyers, whose high-handed behaviour was now resented by the staff. In 1919 the old buyer-dominated Staff Council was replaced by two separate bodies: a Staff Council and a Buyers' Council. Two years later Sir Woodman introduced individual wage packets, so that wage levels in departments were no longer decided by the buyers.

Woodman fulfilled his father's promise to support staff returning from war service. A fund of £10,000 was set up to help those Harrods employees who had been wounded; another £5000 was allotted to ex-soldiers returning to work in the store. Wage increases were granted to all.

None of this is to imply that Sir Woodman's attitude towards his staff did not remain essentially patriarchal. He perhaps lacked the winning charm of his father and could sometimes be brusque and impatient. 'He'd press the button on his desk,' claimed one employee, remembering his days as an office boy, 'and he expected you in the office virtually before his finger was off it. That's what the other boys didn't like, you wanted to be in there quick or you'd get barked at.'

The dress regulations for the staff were strict. The assistants were required to wear black jackets, striped trousers, black shoes and spats. The present ownership, wishing to return to the highest standards—but with sensible concessions to contemporary taste—restated and clarified the dress code for all members of staff in 1993, with the result that Harrods staff are again Britain's smartest retailers.

Their working dress may have changed, but Harrods staff have always been smartly turned out.
LEFT: *Dress code, 1920s;*
RIGHT: *Dress code, 1990s.*

Harrods advertisements
have long been a familiar
sight on London's famous
double-decker buses.
CENTRE: Staff pose
for the camera on their way
to a fancy dress party
at the Harrodian Club
in the early 1920s.

WEATHERING THE STORM

In 1919 — the year the photographer Bedford Lemere recorded
the interior of the store — Harrods achieved a record sales
increase of over £1,850,000. But difficult years followed this short-
lived post-war boom, and Sir Woodman needed a steady
nerve. By 1921 decreasing trade was causing a drop in profits.
The payroll of £3000 a day had somehow to be reduced.
The choice was between cutting staff and cutting wages.
He chose the latter. The store — which until then had refused to
sell cheaply to attract custom, preferring to offer exclusive goods
and first-class service — was forced to get rid of surplus stock
by reducing prices.

The year 1921 brought other changes as well.
The Chairman, Sir Alfred Newton, collapsed and died while
getting out of his car to enter the store. He was then succeeded
by Sir Woodman who remained Managing Director. The new
General Manager was Frank Chitham, who had come from
Selfridges in 1917 to join the managerial team as Merchandise
Manager and Chief of Staff. There was still a Burbidge in
command, but under Sir Woodman the running of the store no
longer depended so much on the genius and vision of a single
individual, as it had in his father's day.

At this time, too, the store lost its apostrophe and
became 'Harrods Limited'.

ADJUSTING TO THE TIMES

Although trade improved only gradually during the early 1920s,
the nature of that trade changed considerably. These were the
Roaring Twenties: the era of short skirts, bobbed hair, sports cars,
cocktails, tea dances and jazz. Without losing the custom of its
more mature, long-established clientele, Harrods had to cater for
contemporary tastes. The flapper became no less important
than the dowager, the Bright Young Thing as valuable as the
peppery Boer War colonel. Harrods managed this, as it managed
most things, superlatively. Without losing a shred of its dignity or
opulence, it coped with changing fashions and attitudes.

New departments were opened, new services offered.
Among the more exotic was the aviation department which
not only sold aeroplanes and flying boats and built hangars,
but also offered flying lessons.

*OPPOSITE: Harrods News
in the 1920s reflected the
changed fashions for more
independent-minded women
in the post-war world.*

*In the 1920s
Harrods could sell
you an aeroplane
and teach you how
to fly it: a page
from the 1929
general catalogue.*

HARRODS AVIATION DEPARTMENT
Join Harrods Flying School and Fly Your Own 'Plane

De Havilland 'Gypsy Moth' Aeroplane
The Best Light Aeroplane in the World

ALL TYPES OF MACHINES ARE AVAILABLE AT HARRODS

Fly in Comfort and Safety   *The 'Gypsy Moth' Seaplane*

HARRODS WILL TAKE YOUR CAR IN PART EXCHANGE

HARRODS LTD   LONDON SW1

HARRODS NEWS
September 17th 1928

For Particulars of Seal Skin Shoes — See Page 3

HARRODS NEWS

Old World Maps Inspire New Paris Tea Gowns!

HARRODS NEWS
February 21st, 1927

New Modes in Motoring Coats

Harrods News
March 3rd 1930.

Spring Fashion Opening

EMPIRE NUMBER
HARRODS NEWS

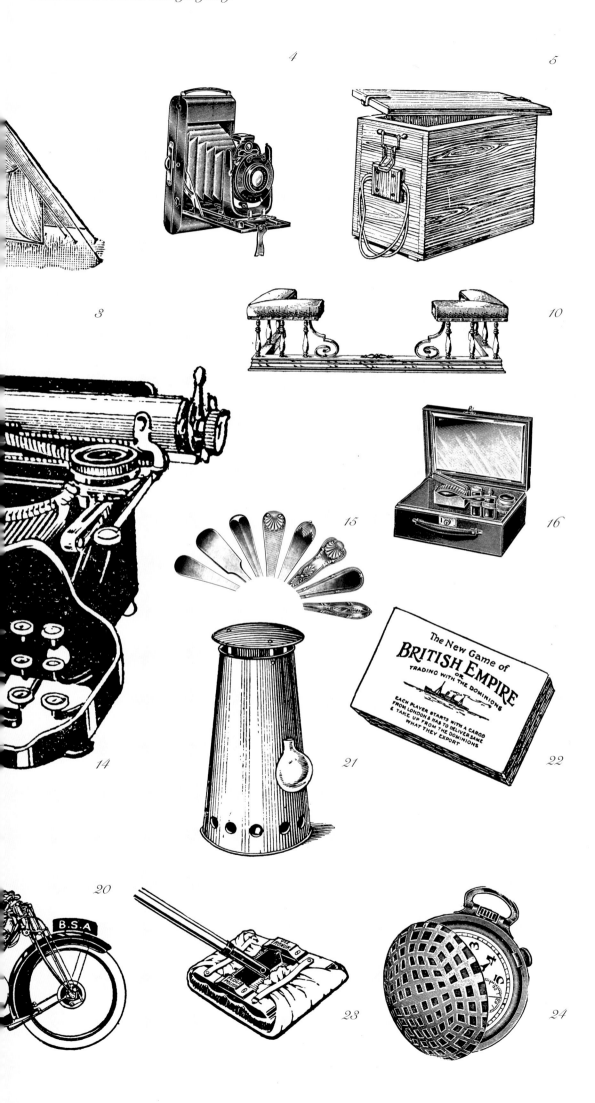

Harrods general catalogues are a treasure trove for social historians. Here are just a few items from the 1929 edition.

CLOCKWISE FROM TOP LEFT:
(1) Children's Model Car; (2) 'Kyrop' Foot Bath; (3) 'Squatters' Tent; (4) Ensign Carbide Camera (tropical model); (5) Ice Conveyor; (6) Megaphone; (7) Harrods Knife Cleaner (8) Lemon Squeezer; (9) Shingle Cap (crocheted silk); (10) Polished Brass Seat Kerb; (11) Harrods 'Super Racket' tennis racket; (12) 'Bronco' Toilet Paper; (13) Wardrobe Brush; (14) 'Coronet' Portable Typewriter; (15) Patterns for Electro-Plate Spoons and Forks; (16) Leather Party Case, with enamelled fittings; (17) Butler's Tray; (18) Ciné-Kodak Model A Motion Picture Camera; (19) Earthernware Spaniel Bowl; (20) B.S.A. Model L28 Motorcycle; (21) Hearson's Patent Egg-Testing Lamp; (22) 'British Empire' board game; (23) 'Ronuk' Home Polisher; (24) Golfer's Watch; (25) Chauffeur's Mackintosh Coat.

The various satellite buildings around the main store —
in Trevor Square, Pentagon Place, Pavilion Road — provided
space for small factories and workshops: the staff now included
architects, cycle repairers, dispensers, engravers, furriers, jewellers,
lace-makers, milliners, opticians, printers, sausage-makers,
upholsterers and watch-makers.

The store's new slogan, 'Get it at Harrods',
was not just an advertising gimmick; whatever it might be,
you could get it at Harrods.

The 1920s saw a steady increase in selling space.
New food departments were built over the old delivery yard.
They lacked the exuberance of the Edwardian interiors, but still
had decorative Doulton tiles. In 1924 the apartments on the
second floor were commandeered for new departments; four years
later, the third floor was similarly taken over, and Sir Woodman,
who had moved into his father's flat, number 51 Hans Mansions,
had to vacate it. He moved up a floor but kept the same number.

The company was expanding in other ways as well.
Between 1919 and 1928 Harrods took over various department
stores, including Kendal Milne in Manchester and D.H. Evans
in Oxford Street, which were to form the Harrods Group.

Indeed, with the benefits flowing from this
expansion and the gradual improvement in trade (the July sales
of 1925 topped £350,000) Sir Woodman Burbidge was able to
request the settlement of a bet that he had made in 1917.
It had been with none other than Gordon Selfridge. 'Wagered Mr
Woodman Burbidge,' wrote Selfridge at the time, 'that within six
(6) years of the declaration of peace we would overtake and pass
Harrods Limited in annual returns. The stake is to be a silver
miniature replica of the loser's store.'

So in 1927, eight years after the official ending
of the war, Sir Woodman wrote to Gordon Selfridge to point
out that far from having passed Harrods in annual returns,
Selfridges had not even drawn level. He asked for the promised
silver replica, but indicated that he would like it to be of
Harrods rather than of Selfridges. Gordon Selfridge agreed.
The replica was made in Harrods silver workshop in Trevor
Square. By kind permission of Lady Benita Burbidge,
this model — a symbol of the good-natured rivalry between
the two stores — stands in Harrods to this day.

Dress-making in the fashion workshop, late 1930s.
BELOW: *Blending tea and roasting coffee, 1960.*

Harrods factories were located in Trevor Square and other buildings near the store. RIGHT: *The bakery, 1930s.* BELOW: *A clock-maker at work* BOTTOM: *The silver factory, 1929. The electroplating workshop.*

TOP LEFT: *The shoe factory, 1930s.* ABOVE: *Making trunks and suitcases, 1930s.* LEFT: *Packing goods for despatch in the basement of the Trevor Square building, 1930s.*

All Harrods saddles are made in Walsall, the industrial home of saddlery, using only the finest saddle butts. They come in a range of fittings designed to suit most horses, and to suit all pursuits, from jumping, general-purpose and polo saddles, to the cheaper synthetic saddle for children.

Customers can try out a selection on the department's 'horse'. The Saddler will then bring these to the stable, where they can be fitted. This service is free within a thirty-mile radius of London, though the Saddler has been known to travel as far afield as Yorkshire. All saddles are sold with a guarantee, and Harrods will restuff and repair old saddles originally bought from the store.

Although today no saddles are made on the premises, the Saddler receives many requests for handmade bridles, which have plain or fancy-stitch nose bands. It takes about five hours to make a plain snaffle, much longer for an elaborate Weymouth. An experienced rider himself, the Saddler can give advice on which sort of bridle or bit is most appropriate for each individual horse.

The workshop also has a traditional treadle-operated boot-patching machine with which repairs can be undertaken on old boots. New rubber boots can be shortened free of charge while you wait, and leather boots let out or fitted with brown hunting tops or patent showjumping cuffs.

Emblazoned on the door of the Master Saddler's workshop, are the three silver feathers of the Prince of Wales's warrant. Established in 1976, Harrods specialist riding department is situated among the sports departments on the fifth floor.

Behind the wooden door, Harrods Master Saddler formerly of the Household Cavalry, makes bridles and fits, services and repairs saddles using traditional awls, pricking irons and tools. If a horse is particularly narrow or wide, the Saddler will takes its measurements, make up a pattern and order a special saddle to be made at no extra cost.

the perfect saddle

the perfect piano

Since it first opened on 12 October 1894, Harrods Piano Department has sold over 74,500 pianos and still maintains the tradition of recording each sale in a series of leather-bound volumes.

Today the department stocks probably the largest range of new pianos anywhere in the country, from the finest Bösendorfers, Bechsteins and Blüthners, to digital pianos and electronic keyboards. To mark its centenary, the department not only sponsored a touring opera and a series of piano recitals at the Wigmore Hall, but also commissioned a collection of four compact discs from pianist Gary Foster and the Royal Philharmonic Orchestra.

The piano buyer, like his twelve sales assistants, has a musical background and plays each piano before buying it for Harrods. Any that do not meet his high standards will be returned to the factory. Most factories, however, 'voice' each piano specially for Harrods and will also make pianos to a customer's specifications, even colour-matching woods to suit existing furniture.

The buyer pays regular visits to piano factories all over the world, travelling as far afield as Japan and Korea. In eastern Germany the new political climate has meant that small, traditional factories are now able to import high-quality parts and produce some superb instruments. But the buyer is equally keen to support the Welmar piano factory in Clapham, now the only wholly British-owned piano manufacturer.

The majority of Harrods customers will be buying an instrument for the first time, so the sales staff take care to ensure that they buy the piano that best suits their needs. Musicians themselves, they want the customer to be happy with the instrument, and as a guarantee of good quality, every piano is sold with a seven-year Harrods warranty, two years longer than a usual guarantee.

To assist the increasing number of customers interested in digital pianos and electronic keyboards, the department employs two computer experts who keep up with the rapidly changing technology.

THE HARRODS KNOW-HOW

A WORLD APART

By now Harrods had generations of loyal customers.
Eric Newby, in his memoirs, *A Traveller's Life*, vividly recalls
his visits to Harrods as a child in the twenties, when he was
taken on shopping expeditions by his mother, a passionate
devotee of the store:

> To me Harrods was not a shop. It was, apart from being
> the place where I had my hair cut, a whole fascinating world, entirely separate
> from the one that I normally inhabited. It was a world that, although finite in its
> extent (it covered thirteen acres), I never explored completely, never could,
> because although at the early age of which I am writing I did not realize this,
> it was one in which fresh vistas were constantly being revealed, and the
> management either opened up new, sometimes ephemeral departments or
> introduced innovations within existing ones.

Newby attributes his love of travel to these early
forays into Harrods, when he would be led through the jungles of
Drapery, past the mountains of the Food Halls, and across
the Arctic wastes of the Linen Department and the deserts of the
Furniture Department.

By the time of the store's seventy-fifth anniversary
celebrations, held in 1924, Harrods could lay claim to a dazzling
new set of statistics. The store boasted 800 telephones and
520 typewriters; each year it received 10,000 letters, used 78
million gallons of water and consumed 3 million units of
electricity. There were no less than 71 freight lifts.

Ambitious building work began in 1929, but the
Wall Street crash ushered in the Depression and brought another
lean period for the store. Trade decreased, profits fell and not
even the stocking of inexpensive merchandise in every
department could increase the takings. Some expansionist
projects had to be shelved. Sir Woodman was even obliged to
introduce the extremely unpopular measure whereby members of
staff were instructed to take an extra week's, unpaid leave.

AN ADVERTISING COUP

In an effort to give languishing trade a boost, even before the
crash, Harrods Advertising Department approached Britain's
three most eminent contemporary men of letters — Arnold
Bennett, H.G. Wells and Bernard Shaw — with a request that

ARNOLD BENNETT and HARRODS

"I will not flout public opinion"

Recently Harrods ventured to invite three of our greatest Masters of the Written Word to lend the influence of their pens to the cause of Business. By permission, and without comment, Harrods publish their replies. The first—that of Mr. Arnold Bennett—appears below:

I HAVE now fully considered your proposal that I should write, for the purposes of publicity, a signed article or series of articles dealing with such aspects of your business as might, on examination, especially appeal to me. I note that you would wish to give me a free hand as to both selection and treatment of topics, and that in particular you are quite ready to accept and to print adverse criticism as well as favourable criticism.

You remind me that, as is well known, your business is among the largest, most comprehensive, and most famous of its kind in the world. You say that it counts notably in the industrial and mercantile life of the community, that your regular staff comprises an immense and constantly increasing number of citizens of both sexes, and that you use every honest endeavour to be of commercial service to the community.

You say further that you buy the best available materials and commodities that research can procure, and that you employ the best organisers, technicians, artists, designers, architects, and craftsmen of every sort that you can discover.

Lastly, you suggest that you ought to be able to enlist the help of descriptive writers in the same category of excellence and prestige as your finest workers in the applied arts.

On my side I will now tell you that as a writer I have always been keenly interested in the very impressive phenomenon of the big departmental store, regarded either as a picturesque spectacle, or as a living organism, or as a sociological portent. I am all in favour of the departmental store. I cannot keep my eyes off its window-displays, its crowds of customers, its army of employees. In Britain, America, France, and Germany I have studied its functioning as far as is possible to an outsider. As a theme for description it strongly appeals to me. I have written articles about it, and I have written a novel entirely about it. That novel, published many years ago, was inspired by the mere sight of your own premises when they were first erected.

I agree with you that you ought to be able to enlist the help of whatever writers seem to you to be adequately equipped for the task you would set. I should like, of course under proper conditions, to accept your proposal; and I see no possible reason against my acceptance, except one.

The reason is that public opinion in Britain is not yet ripe to approve the employment of responsible imaginative writers to whom it has granted a reputation, in any scheme of publicity for a commercial concern. Personally I differ from public opinion in this matter; but the opinion exists and I will not flout it. In flouting it I should certainly lose caste, and I do not intend to lose caste by attempting to create a precedent which could result, for me, in nothing save a disadvantageous notoriety. The time must inevitably come, sooner or later, when the precedent will be created, and after it is established people will wonder why it should ever have met with opposition. But the creator of the precedent will not be myself.

I must therefore, with lively regret, decline your proposal.

Arnold Bennett

Harrods Ltd London SW1

Harrods has always been known for its advertising. This series of newspaper advertisements in 1929, featuring letters written by some of Britain's leading authors, was a celebrated example.

MARCH 5, 1929.

d HARRODS

to be the reader"

each 'lend the influence of their pens in the cause of Business'; in other words, that they write an advertisement for Harrods. All three refused. But in refusing, each wrote long letters giving their reasons. The irrepressible Shaw's letter extended to a thousand words. Literature, they all proclaimed, could never be sullied in such a fashion.

The pontifical air of these refusals was somewhat diluted by the fact that the writers gave Harrods permission to print them. Adroitly, the Advertising Department converted these letters of refusal into three striking advertisements, complete with banner headlines and pictures of the writers, published in the national press in March 1929. Thus, as the Harrods house journal, the *Harrodian Gazette*, put it, 'the honour of literature was preserved and the purity of what Harrods termed 'three of our great "Masters of the Written Word" remained unsullied.' The advertisements won an award.

A NEW IMAGE

The Man's Shop, which opened at the rear of the building in 1929, marked a new departure. Designed by the Harrods Architect, Louis D. Blanc, the exterior along Basil Street was in a distinctive classical style, which owed much to the American Beaux-Arts manner. It was faced with faience, which resembled the familiar Harrodian terracotta, with glazed polychrome decoration in the Harrods colours, green and gold. Inside, instead of separate departments linked by doorways like those along the Brompton Road front, there was a single vast space running the width of the store. On the floors above, the old flats were replaced by shop

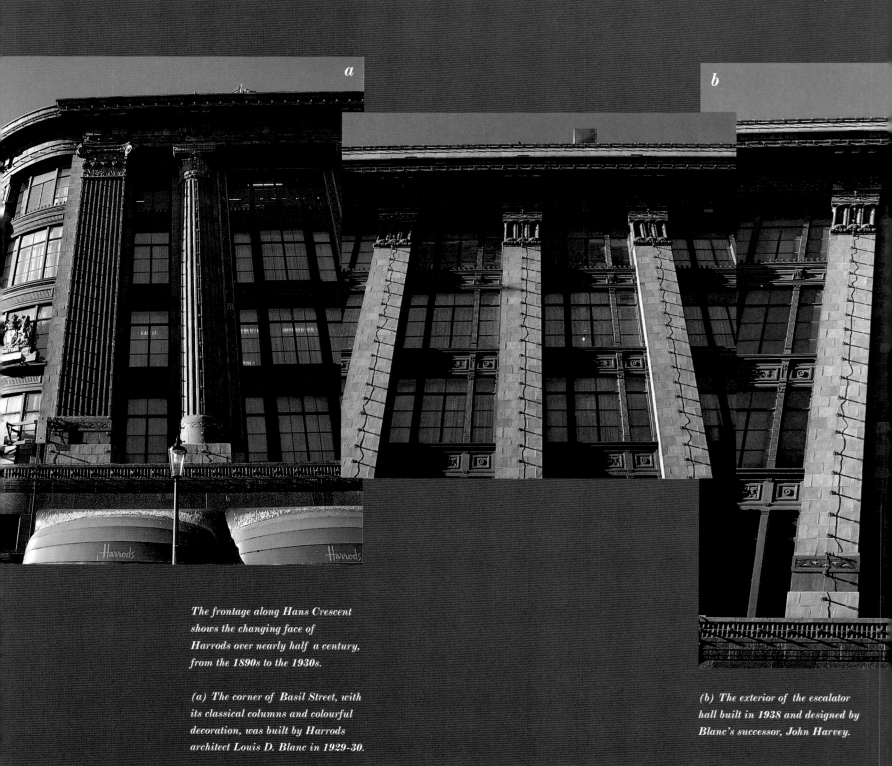

The frontage along Hans Crescent shows the changing face of Harrods over nearly half a century, from the 1890s to the 1930s.

(a) The corner of Basil Street, with its classical columns and colourful decoration, was built by Harrods architect Louis D. Blanc in 1929-30.

(b) The exterior of the escalator hall built in 1938 and designed by Blanc's successor, John Harvey.

space. In the basement a new barber shop was opened. Its decoration brought transatlantic Art Deco to the store, while its lounge — today the 'Green Man' pub — was redolent of an Old English manor house.

A bank of eight new lifts was installed, taking the total number of passenger lifts to over thirty. The Georgian Restaurant was extended and given its elegant Art Deco sky-light, while nearby, the now vanished Silver Buffet, with its silver walls and tubular steel furniture, showed that the store was in tune with the latest modern style.

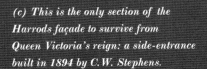

(c) This is the only section of the Harrods façade to survive from Queen Victoria's reign: a side-entrance built in 1894 by C.W. Stephens.

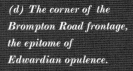

(d) The corner of the Brompton Road frontage, the epitome of Edwardian opulence.

Not until 1932 did the Depression begin to lift. The subsequent upturn in sales enabled the delayed improvements to be put in hand. The fourth floor at the front of the building was taken over, allowing for the opening of a new Hair and Beauty Salon — the biggest in Europe — and a splendid suite of offices for the directors and management. Work on the rebuilding of the central block was completed in 1936. The project was begun by Louis Blanc and completed by his successor as Harrods House Architect, John Harvey. The new, larger Banking Hall (located where the Cosmetics Hall is today), reflecting the more restrained taste of the mid-1930s, replaced the neo-Baroque ceilings, scrolled ironwork and mahogany counters of the old banking hall, the Royal Exchange. This was cleared to become the Central Exhibition Hall. Instead of the array of richly coloured marbles there was plain, golden-coloured travertine stone. Not that it was any less luxurious: the effect was still of grandeur and, like its Edwardian predecessor, it had a rubber-tiled floor ensuring the necessary atmosphere of dignified discretion.

*The stylish new Banking Hall
shortly after its completion in 1934.
(The clockface shows that this
photograph was taken before the
store opened for business;
the 'customers' lounging elegantly
in the green armchairs are in
fact members of staff.)*

EVENTS

Throughout the twenties and thirties, Harrods continued its remarkable programme of special promotions, exhibitions and events. The orchestral concert in 1909 proved the first of many. World-famous conductors, such as Sir Thomas Beecham and Sir Henry Wood, were invited to bring their orchestras to the store to give free performances. There were also recitals by leading soloists.

One of the most celebrated exhibitions ever held in the store took place in 1934, when Harrods demonstrated its commitment to modern art and design by showing an array of household ceramics and glass with designs specially commissioned from some of the most famous British artists of the day.

LEFT: *Among the artists' ceramics exhibited at Harrods in 1934 perhaps the wittiest was Dame Laura Knight's circus plate.*
BELOW: *Sir Woodman Burbidge shows art critic John Rothenstein round the exhibition. A great variety of artists took part, including Graham Sutherland, Ben Nicholson and Duncan Grant. Some designs can be seen here.*

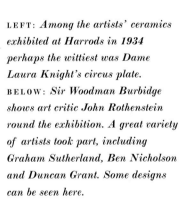

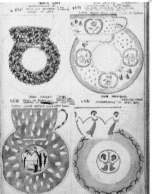

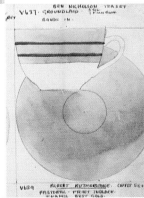

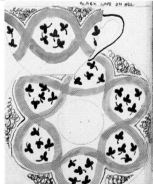

PNEUMATIC CASH

One of the most impressive innovations of the mid-thirties was the pneumatic tube system. Richard Burbidge had introduced a smaller tube system around the turn of the century, but the installation, in 1934, of one that extended throughout the building was a major undertaking. The pneumatic tubes, made by the Lanson Company, carried cash — and on a separate system internal messages — through the store. Customers' money, placed in a carrier in the tube, was whisked at 17 miles per hour down to the central cash tube room in the basement. Here cashiers extracted the money, put the correct change back into the carrier, adjusted the destination number and sent it whizzing back. The Harrods tube system was claimed to be the most extensive in the British Empire, with 39 miles of twisting pipes. The longest journey — a quarter of a mile — took a mere 54 seconds.

Only occasionally were there mishaps in the tube system. As recently as the mid-1960s one inexperienced temporary salesgirl put sixty-four pound notes straight into the tube and not, as was essential, into the carrier. Within seconds the cashiers in the basement were being showered with sixty-four shredded one pound notes. Not until the 1970s did the volume of trade and the advent of new technology render the tube system obsolete.

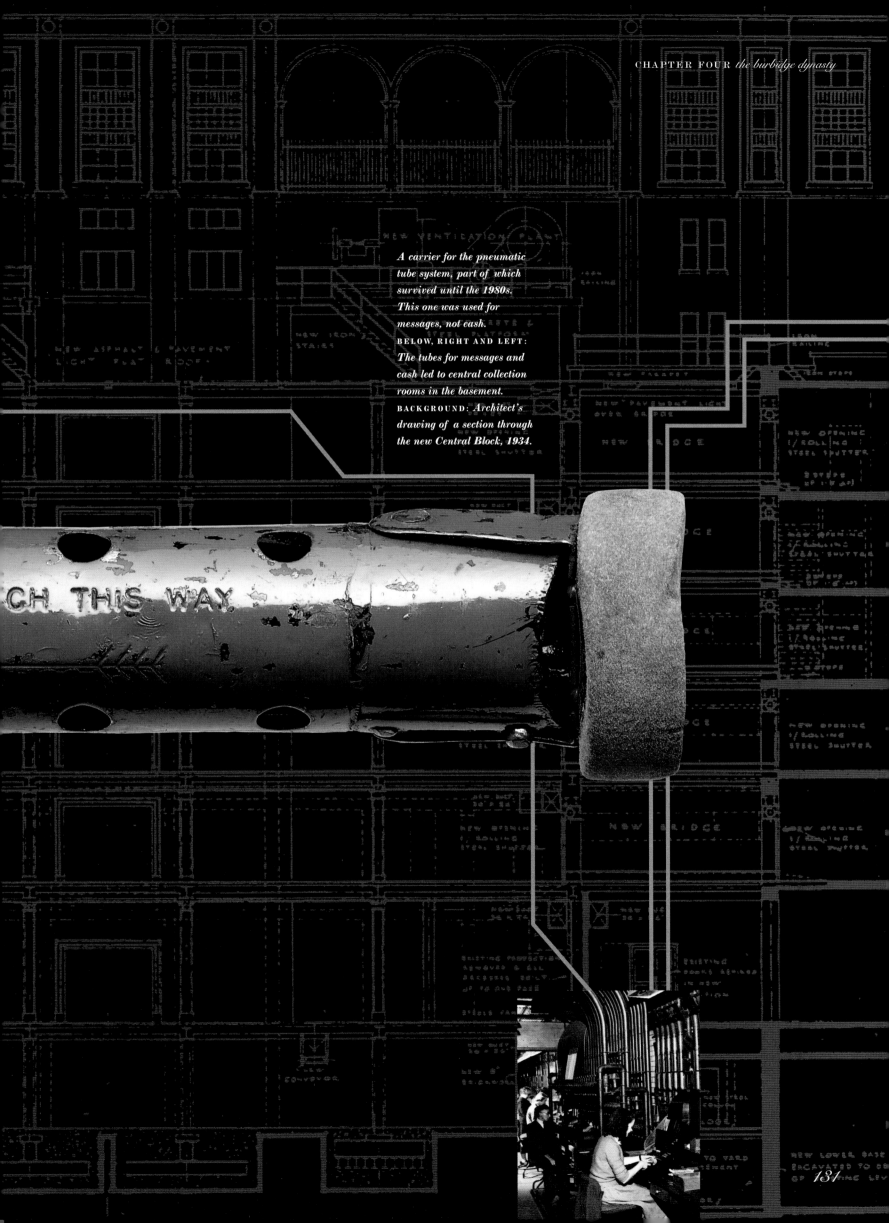

A carrier for the pneumatic tube system, part of which survived until the 1980s. This one was used for messages, not cash.
BELOW, RIGHT AND LEFT: *The tubes for messages and cash led to central collection rooms in the basement.*
BACKGROUND: *Architect's drawing of a section through the new Central Block, 1934.*

By 1935, when Sir Woodman Burbidge decided to retire as
Managing Director, the number of people working at Harrods had
reached its peak. There was a staff of 7000, of which 3000 were
sales staff, 2000 in workrooms and factories, 1000 in
administration and 1000 in services such as catering and
hairdressing. Considering that Sir Woodman had been obliged to
run the store during one of the most turbulent economic and
social periods in recent history, his achievements had been
remarkable. His shrewdness, industry and sound business sense
were more suited to the times than his father's somewhat
buccaneering style. Although no longer Managing Director,
Sir Woodman remained as Chairman for a further ten years.
He died, at the age of seventy-five, in 1945.

A THIRD GENERATION

'My love of this business,' the second Sir Richard Burbidge once
commented, 'was instilled into me ever since I was a boy of five
and my grandfather used to take me over the scaffolding at the
back of Hans Road.'

    That had been in 1902 when the expansion of
Harrods was in full flood. Young Richard Burbidge could never
have doubted that he would one day inherit the responsibility for
the running of this gigantic commercial enterprise. He was
groomed for it from the start. Having received his schooling at
Rugby and served in the First World War, Richard Burbidge
was sent, at the age of twenty-one, to the United States where,
at the famous Wanamakers, he was taught the basics of the retail
trade. He joined Harrods in 1920 as Assistant Merchandise
Manager under Frank Chitham. In 1927 he became General
Manager and, on the retirement of his father in 1935,
Managing Director. Richard Burbidge was thirty-eight.

    A good-looking man, of great kindness and courtesy,
Mr Richard, as he was known (not until his father's death in 1945
did he inherit the title), brought a gratifyingly human touch to
his dealings with the staff. Young Richard Burbidge had inherited
his grandfather's amiability, but without his autocratic character;
he was never anything less than charming. 'He used to come down
to the despatch office and wish us a happy Christmas,'
remembered one employee, 'there would be over a hundred men
there and he would know every one of them by name.' When one
remembers that the staff numbered 7000 at the time — and that

*For many years Harrods ran an
annual handwriting competition
for youngsters. Here Richard
Burbidge presents the trophy to its
proud winners in 1934.*
OPPOSITE: *Mr Richard's memory
for the names of his staff was
legendary. The photograph
of the Managing Director on his
bicycle was taken during the
Second World War.*

"Have a Merry Christmas Mr Harvey, Mr Lamb,
Mr Peters, Mr Pollard, Mr Maddison, Mr Banks,
Mr Harrap, Mr Eardly, Mr Gearing, Mr Leathers,
Mr Reynolds, Mr Clements, Mr Cook, Mr Gaston,
Mr Dowling, Mr Jordon, Mr Smart, Mr Jones,
Mr Walsh, Mr Wells, Mr Bailey, Mr Yarrow, Mr Good,
Mr Cowan, Mr Turton, Mr Carter, Mr Burrell,
Mr Sharpe, Mr Tuthill, Mr Richardson, Mr Hanson,
Mr Davies, Mr Page, Mr Denton, Mr Sykes,
Mr Hambling, Mr Friend, Mr Graham, Mr Walsh,
Mr Clarke, Mr Watts, Mr Lawrence, Mr Baird,
Mr Gifford, Mr Weston, Mr Redgrave, Mr Hill,
Mr Pugh, Mr Collins, Mr Turner, Mr Humphries,
Mr Everitt, Mr Godfree, Mr Short, Mr Temple,
Mr Shave, Mr Norman, Mr Valentine, Mr Mathews,
Mr Cutting, Mr Macintosh, Mr Dickerson, Mr Potts,
Mr English, Mr Carter, Mr Austin, Mr Parrish,
Mr Hicks, Mr Stevens, Mr Devoy, Mr Sherrin,
Mr Bone, Mr Donnelly, Mr Thatcher,
Mr Jeffrey, Mr Thompson, Mr Royce,
Mr Clift, Mr Simmons, Mr Palmer,
Mr Lesley, Mr Williams, Mr MacDougall,
Mr Marlow, Mr Smith, Mr Martin,
Mr Bruce, Mr Fraser, Mr Adams,
Mr Miln, Mr Luckstop, Mr Halliday,
Mr Baldock, Mr Applebee, Mr Tricker,
Mr Gaston, Mr Hanover, Mr Doyle,
Mr Chamberlain, Mr Appleyard and
Mr MacGregor **and a Happy New Year**"

none of them wore a name badge as they do today — Richard
Burbidge's talent for remembering names is astounding.
It was the sort of thing that made him popular with the staff.

One retired employee has a revealing story.
'I well remember one morning when Sir Richard Burbidge was
walking through the department and he stopped and said to me,
"Have you received the letter I sent down to you Mr Sharpe?".
"No, Sir Richard," I replied. "Well, its on its way. She [the
customer] doesn't think much of you, four pages of it . . ."

*The elegant ambiance of the
Younger Set Gown Department,
photographed a few years after
its opening in 1934.*
OPPOSITE: *The new escalator
hall, with Harrods' first
escalators since 1898, was
opened in 1939, completing
the store's rebuilding
programme a few months before
war broke out.*

'The letter duly arrived, all four pages and, last of other things, threatening court action. It really was a shocker ... Well, with the help of my buyer, Mr Gifford, a full report was typed out and sent to Sir Richard's office. There was nothing else I could do but wait. Next day I was handed Sir Richard's reply. I couldn't believe my eyes. He was returning the customer's money in full, with a request to her not to enter his store again. He would not have his staff compromised and intimidated in this way. A few days later when Sir Richard was walking through he said to me, "Have you read my letter, Sharpe?" " Yes, Sir," I said, full of smiles. He slightly turned to go away then, as an afterthought, turned and said, "Do you feel better now?"'

Because much of his period in office was overshadowed by the Second World War and the years of austerity that followed it, Richard Burbidge was able to initiate few major developments in the store.

Before the war he presided over the completion of the alterations begun by his father. The last of the old building in the centre of the store was demolished and new showrooms built around a central staircase. They included fashion and furniture showrooms, a lounge and writing room for customers, an enquiry office and interviewing rooms.

The most impressive of Richard Burbidge's own building projects was the creation of a spacious hall mid-way along the Hans Crescent side of the building, which was completed in 1939. This housed a new set of escalators capable of carrying 20,000 customers an hour. They were the first escalators to be installed since the moving staircase caused such a stir in 1898. They remained the only escalators in the building until 1981.

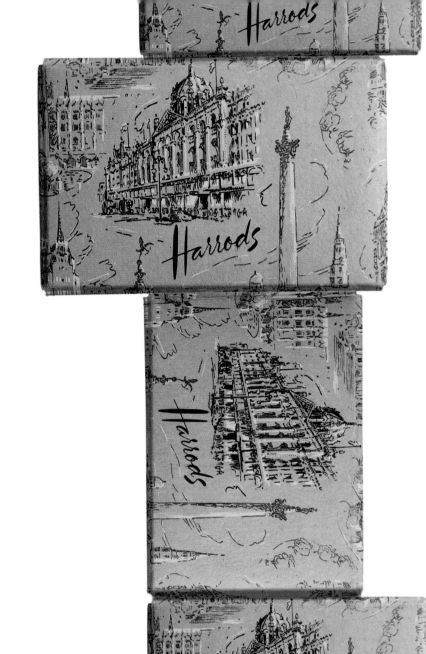

1950s

1920s

1930s

BAGS OF DISTINCTION

A minor but not insignificant move at this time was the introduction of carrier bags in the store's famous dark green and gold (also Sir Woodman Burbidge's racing colours) with the distinctive Harrods logo. At first these were used only during sales. It was a form of advertising in which many of the store's socially-aspiring customers were only too delighted to participate. Many years later Jimmy Carter, the President of the United States, emerged from his plane with a Harrods carrier bag in his hand.

1950s

Harrods bags and boxes are not all green and gold.
LEFT TO RIGHT: *Poultry bag, c. 1925; box, 1930s; boxes decorated with sketches of Harrods with other London landmarks (the design was introduced for the Festival of Britain in 1951); the same design as modified in the 1970s; Way In carrier bag, c. 1970; carrier bag for the 1989 Colourful Harrods promotion; Pharaonic carrier bag for the Egyptian Hall, 1991.*

1970s

1970s

1980s

1990s

'SOCIETY'S FAVOURITE STORE'

In the late 1930s, Harrods was generally regarded as the store which catered for what was still called 'Society'. These were the sunset years of the old aristocratic rituals and Harrods provided services for all the great social events of 'the season': debutante balls, coming-out parties, society weddings, race meetings, exhibition openings, royal garden parties, the Henley Regatta, the Aldershot Tattoo and that important rite of passage for all well-born young ladies: presentation at court. For this particular function, Harrods could supply the clothes, accessories (including the obligatory three ostrich feathers), hair-styles, limousines, chauffeurs and, finally, photographs.

'My first impression of Harrods was its almost garden party atmosphere,' remembered an assistant who joined the store in the summer of 1938. 'The customers were either preparing for Ascot or a Presentation, and their excitement and pleasure seemed to have affected everyone at the store, so that Harrods appeared a very busy and gay place.'

Celebrities were to be seen throughout the store. Lady Furness, close friend of the Prince of Wales, with her twin sister Gloria Vanderbilt once staged and modelled their own fashion show. The Prince of Wales himself — the future King Edward VIII — was a visitor to the exhibitions of Empire produce, which were regularly held in the Central Exhibition Hall. In 1938 the new Queen, consort to King George VI, brought

her young daughters, Princess Elizabeth and Princess Margaret, to do their Christmas shopping. Victor Sylvester, later renowned as the strict-tempo band leader, played for tea dances in the Georgian Restaurant. Noel Coward was one of the many artistes who entertained shoppers in the Piano Department. (Coward was also the recipient of one of the more unusual Christmas presents to have been bought at Harrods: an alligator, given to him by Beatrice Lillie.)

FAR LEFT: *Harrods News announces the impending Piano Sale with a clutch of famous musicians, 1929.*
LEFT: *Ladies' fashions through the decades, from 1915 to the 1950s.*

Harrods has supplied dressing-gowns (and other clothing) to the discerning man since the 1890s. The image of Harrods customers depicted in the catalogues changed remarkably little from the turn of the century to the 1950s.

HARRODS FIFTEEN GRADUA

Harrods
Range of Fifteen
**GRADUATED
SIZES**
IN
FASHION GARMENTS
is by far the most
complete in the Kingdom

Harrods
Range of Fifteen
**GRADUATED
SIZES**
IN
FASHION GARMENTS
is by far the most
complete in the Kingdom

HARRODS
Wonderful Values in Coats

*A Harrods fashion
department caters for all
shapes and sizes of
customer, as this
photograph from 1930
clearly demonstrates.
Many of Harrods'
innovations in fashion
retailing, such as
informative labels about
fabric care, were to
become standard.*

If you are any
of these
FIFTEEN
SIZES
Harrods can fit you
perfectly with your
Fashion Garments
from stock

THE SECOND WORLD WAR

The outbreak of war in 1939 had a profound effect on the store. The patriotism of management and staff, so evident during the Boer War and the First World War, was again beyond question. But this time the civilian population of Britain — including, of course, the Harrods' staff — was involved even more than it had been in 1914-1918. Almost 1900 employees saw active service, while almost every member of staff was somehow or other caught up in the war effort.

A ton and a half of cardboard was used to block up the windows and 18,000 sandbags were filled and humped into place by the staff. An Air Raid Protection unit was formed and the basement converted into an air-raid shelter. Fire pickets were on duty throughout the war, with the staff working on a rota basis and sleeping in either the basement or the Georgian restaurant. A reinforced-concrete pill box for spotting enemy aircraft was erected on the highest point of the roof, with narrow observation slits in the walls and a direct telephone link with the control room in the basement. It was manned by two 'spotters' armed with binoculars. At a formal ceremony it was named, in mock tribute to Hitler's mountain hideaway, 'Berchtesgaden'.

Fortunately, the main building emerged largely unscathed from the Blitz, the only serious damage to the main building being the destruction of the recently completed Hair and Beauty Salon by an incendiary bomb. However, in 1944, a doodlebug completely devastated the Harrods Estate Offices across Brompton Road.

Trade fell off badly. What with petrol rationing, fewer train services and the retreat of so many regular customers to the country or even abroad, there was very little spending being done.

OPPOSITE: Devastation left by the flying-bomb that destroyed Harrods Estate Offices in Brompton Road in 1944. ABOVE: The vigilance of the Air Raid Protection service, here on parade in the escalator hall, prevented serious damage to the main building. BELOW: Mrs Winston Churchill visiting one of the wartime exhibitions, 1944. BOTTOM: Wartime scenes in the store, June 1941: trading continued, but ration coupons were required.

Not that there was much to spend money on: supplies were seriously limited and food and clothes rationed. Shop hours were cut and delivery services curtailed.

But the store was also doing its bit, as it had in the First War. The clothing workrooms were turned over to making uniforms, and the factories produced parachutes by day and parts for Lancaster bombers by night. Harrods vans were requisitioned for army use; some of them saw active service on the North African campaign. As the building had its own power and water supplies, parts of it were taken over by the Royal Navy and the Royal Canadian Air Force.

In 1943 the cookery expert Marguerite Patten joined Harrods to run its Food Advice Service. She had an unenviable job. Not only had many of the society matrons attending her demonstrations never had to cook for themselves before, but she also had to manage on meagre wartime rations: weekly allowances of 2 ounces of butter, 8 ounces of sugar and dried eggs. Nevertheless she remembers the atmosphere as 'one of incredible mateyness.'

Victory in Europe Day in May 1945 was celebrated with as much gusto as the shabby, shuttered store could muster. A massive, five-storey high Victory V was assembled from scrap metal and bolted onto the front of the building and, on a banner stretching for half a block, were lettered the words 'God Save the King'. A queue of loyal customers, anxious to buy something to mark this momentous occasion, stretched round the store from the main Brompton Road entrance as far back as Basil Street.

A week later, the ever-considerate Richard Burbidge sent a message to reassure those members of the staff whose release from active service was to be delayed, that their interests would not suffer and that a bonus of four weeks' wages would be waiting for them.

OPPOSITE: *Bruised but unbowed, the store celebrated Victory in Europe, May 1945.* RIGHT: *Advice on how best to use wartime rations was dispensed by Marguerite Patten and others in the Meat Hall, 1943. Rows of jars are painted on the empty shelves.* BELOW: *After the war, Mrs Patten wrote several recipe books for Harrods.*

A CENTURY
OF ACHIEVEMENT

In 1949 Harrods celebrated its centenary. In the difficult circumstances of post-war austerity the store made the most of the occasion. A model of Charles Henry Harrod's original shop was built in the Central Exhibition Hall, and Sir Richard Burbidge commissioned a commemorative book entitled *A Story of British Achievement*, which was distributed to all members of staff and interested customers.

Among the plethora of statistics published in the Centenary Souvenir were some of abiding interest. Although subsequent inflation may have rendered the sums of money mentioned less impressive, the measurements and quantities remain remarkable. The floor area covered by Harrods, including warehouses, was 35 acres; a million books were borrowed each year from the store's circulating library; 8000 miles of string were used annually; 6000 letters were dispatched every afternoon; 8000 staff meals were served every day.

NEWS, MARCH 1949

In the 1950s there was not much money available for extensive refurbishment or modernization. Alterations to the store were restricted mainly to removing or concealing parts of the now unfashionable Edwardian décor. It was not until the 1980s that many of these were revealed again.

However, the post-war years saw a spectacular growth of the Harrods Group of stores. Since 1913, when Woodman Burbidge had opened Harrods in Buenos Aires, the Harrods empire had grown considerably. In the 1920s, Harrods had acquired and subsequently disposed of Swan & Edgar in Piccadilly, but in the 1950s it still owned D.H. Evans in Oxford Street (acquired in 1928), as well as Kendal Milne and Walter Carter in Manchester. To these were now added a clutch of bomb-damaged provincial stores: Hendersons in Liverpool, John Walsh in Sheffield, Rackhams in Birmingham and J.K. Rockley's two smaller stores in the West Country. Together they formed the fifth-largest department store group in Great Britain, with Harrods as the incomparable jewel in the crown.

FRED
TAYLOR

An artist's impression of Harrods, bedecked for the
Coronation. Unique in size, in luxury, in century-old
tradition and, above all, in the scope and quality of
its goods and services, it is London's most famous store.

ABOVE: *The Brompton Road
frontage, as depicted by artist
Fred Taylor for the store's
centenary book, 1949.*
LEFT: *Coronation decorations,
June 1953.*

149

'THE BATTLE OF KNIGHTSBRIDGE'

This burgeoning brought its dangers.
The desirable group was becoming a prime
target for a take-over bid. When, in 1958, it
became known that the company's properties
had been revalued at £20 million on an
issued capital of only £8 million, Harrods
was revealed as extremely vulnerable.
Fully aware of this, Sir Richard Burbidge
made overtures to Debenhams, at that
time the largest group of stores in the
country, to discuss the possibility of a merger.

It was at this stage that the redoubtable Glaswegian
store-owner, Hugh Fraser, entered the scene. Since 1948, when his
group of stores had become a public company, Hugh Fraser had
developed into a formidable exponent of the take-over. By 1957
he had established a foothold in London with the acquisition of
John Barkers, Derry & Toms, and Pontings, the main stores in

The Harrods take-over saga
gripped the nation in 1959,
making headline news.
For the Scottish store-owner
Hugh Fraser (ABOVE LEFT,
AND RIGHT), Harrods was to
be the flagship of his House of
Fraser retailing empire.

Kensington High Street, just down the road from Harrods. Two years later he turned his attention to the most prestigious prize in British retailing.

Hugh Fraser's epic campaign to gain control of Harrods became known in the City as 'The Battle of Knightsbridge'. The detail in which the battle was reported in the daily press was an indication of both the importance that Harrods had in national life and the affection in which the store was held by the general public. 'This financial battle', reported one astonished French journalist, 'is being followed by the English with the same interest which they normally reserve for the sports results.'

The campaign was complicated by the fact that it was a three-cornered one: between Debenhams, the House of Fraser and the giant United Drapery Stores. Hugh Fraser, who was actually in the least favourable financial position, fought with his customary nerve, skill and tenacity. The first to withdraw from the field was Joseph Collier of the United Drapery Stores. He sold his shares to Fraser. Debenhams, after a further show of resistance, finally conceded defeat. In September 1959 Hugh Fraser presided over his first board meeting as Chairman of Harrods. The Harrods Group was now part of the House of Fraser.

This marked, of course, the end of the road for Sir Richard Burbidge. Although in the difficult post-war period the store inevitably lacked something of it earlier dynamism and was in need of modernization and investment, Sir Richard had worked tirelessly for the good of Harrods. The reports he wrote on his regular visits to the United States, reveal not only his keen perception of political and economic trends but also his awareness of the great changes taking place in the retail trade.

He made no secret of his resentment of the House of Fraser take-over and there were many in the business world who felt deep sympathy for him. He stayed on for a few months and his departure, in 1960, meant that for the first time in nearly seventy years, Harrods did not have a Burbidge in command.

Hugh Fraser took a close interest in the fortunes of the store which was his most prestigious acquisition, but he entrusted the day-to-day running of it to others. Inevitably, Harrods was to go though a period of great turbulence, as well as great commercial expansion.

COLOUR, STYLE AND MOVING TRENDS

LEFT: *Ever alert,*
Harrods observed
the new shopping
habits of the 1960s
(self selection and
a preference for
exclusive small
outlets) and came
up with an answer.
The Way In
boutique was
launched in 1967.

he Burbidges in their different ways
had all run Harrods along paternalistic
lines. Living in their flat above the store,
all members of the Burbidge family
had been drawn into the Harrodian
world. In 1975 Mrs Enid Venables,
one of Sir Woodman's daughters
recalled: 'We had innumerable personal friends among the staff
with whom we exchanged Christmas cards and if retirement
came to any member of the staff, we always went to say good-
bye, a practice I and my sister continue today.' Inevitably, things
would be different with the House of Fraser.

Hugh Fraser died in 1966, having been honoured with a baronetcy and a life peerage. He was succeeded as Chairman by his son, the second Sir Hugh Fraser. However, the actual management of the store was chiefly in the hands, consecutively, of three men: Alfred Spence, Robert Midgley and Aleck Craddock. Each had his own style but together they presided over a period of unprecedented growth. By 1985, the store was taking over £300 million annually.

Alfred Spence was a man of great warmth and tact. Not unnaturally, there was a certain resentment among some long-serving members of the management and staff at this change of ownership. Without ever being anything less than resolute, the new Managing Director handled a potentially difficult situation with admirable sensitivity.

SWINGING HARRODS: WAY IN

The early years of the Fraser period coincided with a period of radical social change. Like the Roaring Twenties, the Swinging Sixties introduced new attitudes, tastes and fashions. There was an emphasis on youth (the young had more money to spend), a collapse of rigid class divisions, a relaxing of sexual taboos and a burgeoning of new talent. It was the age of Carnaby Street, rock music and the mini-skirt. London was at the heart of this change. In Knightsbridge, mews cottages in back-streets were being converted into open-plan residences, while in the King's Road, not far away, a plethora of fashionable 'boutiques' sprang up.

Set against this vibrant scene, Harrods had a decidedly old-fashioned aura. Yet one of the triumphs of this period was the skill with which the store once again adapted to a swiftly changing world.

In the first place, something had to be done to appeal to a younger and more emancipated generation. The solution was provided by the Merchandise Director, Gordon Anthony. With the enthusiastic backing of the new Chairman, the young Sir Hugh Fraser, the whole length of the Fourth Floor on the Basil Street side of the store was to be devoted entirely to young fashion. Opened in 1967, it was the first of London's in-store boutiques, complete with 'trendy' decor, flashing lights and piped music. Its name, chosen by a competition among the staff, was 'Way In'— a play on the fashionable phrase 'way out'.

FROM TOP LEFT:
Harrods delivers to the Beatles. On the Fourth Floor at Harrods there was a magical new young world of the 60s: first Women's Hairdressing was given a new look, and by 1967, Way In had gone for radical change in layout and colour with clothes designed for the revolutionary new styles and body-shape. It must have been as big a shock to the older customers as the Flappers were in the 1920s.

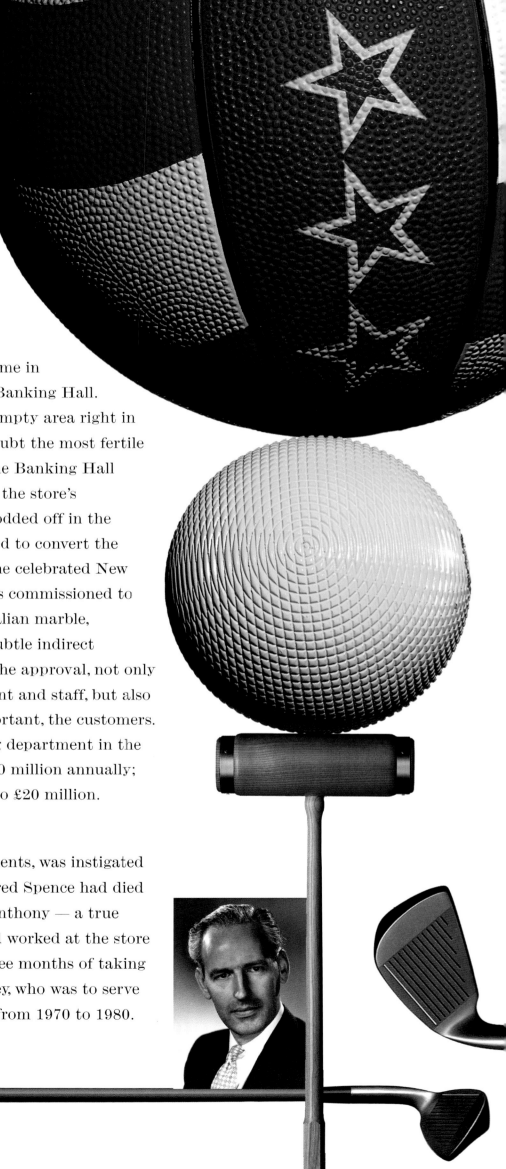

Another adaptation to a changing way of life was instigated in the Food Halls. In the sixties the growth of self-service supermarkets had conditioned customers to a different way of shopping: not all of them wanted to stand at counters waiting to be served. Harrods' answer was to open a section of the Food Halls where customers could help themselves and make a single payment at a cash desk.

An even more radical change came in 1970 with the disappearance of the famous Banking Hall. Since it occupied 11,000 square feet, a vast empty area right in the middle of the ground floor — without doubt the most fertile selling space in Europe — the retention of the Banking Hall was simply no longer viable. To the alarm of the store's traditionalists and the old gentlemen who nodded off in the bank's green leather armchairs, it was decided to convert the area into a perfumery and cosmetics hall. The celebrated New York firm of Copeland, Novak and Israel was commissioned to design the new room. By the use of white Italian marble, red velvet furnishings, island counters and subtle indirect lighting, an interior was created which won the approval, not only of the most die-hard members of management and staff, but also of the perfumery houses and, still more important, the customers. It quickly established itself as the top-selling department in the store. Within ten years, it was taking over £10 million annually; within another ten, it had doubled the sum to £20 million.

ROBERT MIDGLEY

This, and many of the other major developments, was instigated by Robert Midgley. When the diplomatic Alfred Spence had died in 1970, he had been succeeded by Gordon Anthony — a true Harrodian: he, and his father before him, had worked at the store for many years. But sadly, he died within three months of taking up his post. His successor was Robert Midgley, who was to serve as Managing Director (and later Chairman) from 1970 to 1980.

Midgley was a trusted Fraser man of many years standing. A dynamic, industrious and disciplined Scot, he was determined to involve himself in the day-to-day workings of the store. He frequently toured the entire 35 acres of the store and warehouses two or three times a day. Any instruction had to be carried out immediately. He came to Harrods as an outsider but over the years became increasingly attuned to the special character of the store: he became 'Harrodized'.

Midgley's belief in strong, centralized control worked. At the end of his ten-year period, sales figures had increased five-fold. And if some of this increase could be attributed to the effects of inflation, the greater part of it was due to Midgley's vigorous managerial style.

But Napoleon's dictum, that what a successful general needed most was luck, also applied to Robert Midgley. His luck came in the form of the tourist boom which affected London in the seventies, boosted by the devaluation of Britain's currency, and the soaring oil prices which brought so many wealthy Gulf Arabs to London.

He was able to take advantage, too, of the phenomenal growth of leisure activities. Showing the same single-minded resolve that he had demonstrated in sweeping away the Banking Hall, Midgley now got rid of another apparently sacrosanct area: the beautifully oak-panelled suite of management offices and boardroom which had been installed on the fourth floor in the 1930s. It was replaced by the Olympic Way — a superb sports retailing department which proved hardly less successful than the new Perfumery Department.

BOTTOM LEFT:
Robert Midgley, appointed Managing Director in 1970, took a cool look at the layout of the store and decided that every square foot must pay its way. The end had come in 1976 for the luxurious Management offices on the fourth floor which became the new Sports department, the Olympic Way.

BOMBINGS

Twice during the Fraser period, trade was brought to a dramatic halt because of terrorist bombs laid by the IRA. On 21 December 1974, the last Saturday before Christmas when the store was crowded with shoppers, Margaret Fyall, a sales assistant in the House and Garden Tools Department, noticed a small, unattended hold-all. She immediately alerted the security guards. The department was cleared and the fire shutters wound down. The bomb exploded at 5 p.m. Its impact shook the entire building and the department was

completely wrecked. The store was evacuated and closed. Unrequested, staff volunteers streamed in the next day, Sunday, to help clear up the mess. The department was rebuilt and reopened for trade within weeks.

Harrods has learned from the past: vigilance and preparation now ensure safety. ABOVE: Bomb damage in the Garden Tool department, 1974. BELOW: The savage blast which claimed lives in 1983. Within the store forward planning and swift action saved the shoppers.

Almost exactly nine years later — on 17 December 1983 — came a second, more disastrous, terrorist outrage. Again, as in 1974, it was a Saturday and the store packed with Christmas shoppers. This time the bombers issued a warning and the management was faced with the agonising decision as to whether or not the store should be evacuated. Presuming the bomb to be in a car parked outside the store, they decided against evacuation. Calmly but firmly, and using the public address system installed after the previous bombing, the General Manager instructed the customers to move into the centre of the building so that they would be as far away from the expected blast as possible. There is no doubt that this saved countless lives.

At 1.19 p.m., with a thunderous impact, the bomb exploded outside Door No. 4 in Hans Crescent. Five people and a police dog were killed outright and a sixth person died shortly afterwards. There were many other casualties. It was the worst disaster ever to hit the store. Today, a simple memorial marks the spot.

In 1993, Harrods was yet again the target of the IRA. This time an explosive device was placed in a litter bin outside the front of the store in Brompton Road, but the damage was not serious. The insistence of the Chairman, Mohamed Al Fayed, on sophisticated security systems paid off. Thanks to his foresight Harrods had been equipped with one of the most complete closed-circuit television systems to be found in any commercial organization. As a result it was possible to retrieve footage of the device being placed in the litter bin and to identify the culprits. They were arrested, tried and imprisoned.

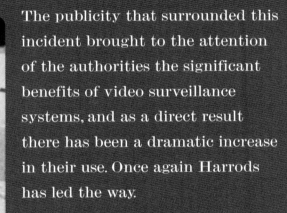

The publicity that surrounded this incident brought to the attention of the authorities the significant benefits of video surveillance systems, and as a direct result there has been a dramatic increase in their use. Once again Harrods has led the way.

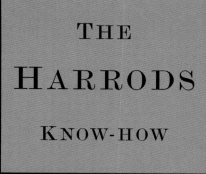

THE HARRODS KNOW-HOW

the perfect pet

Possibly the most famous purchase ever made at Harrods Pet Department was a baby elephant in 1967. Today only British-bred, small breeds of animal are kept, as the department aims, above all else, to ensure that the animals' stay in the store will be a happy one. And since the animals' welfare is paramount, the department will not sell a pet to anyone they do not consider will make a good owner.

Animal lovers like to buy at Harrods because they know that the pet they take home will have received the best care and be in peak condition. To that end, all litters of puppies or kittens are examined by an external vet and must be given a clean bill of health before being shown to customers.

The small-breed puppies include Yorkshire and West Highland Terriers, Cavalier King Charles Spaniels, miniature Schnauzers, Pekinese, Bichon Frisé and Dachshunds, and assistants can recommend breeders of larger dogs. If, however, a particular breed is not in the store, customers can ask to be contacted when it becomes available.

The pets are kept in a closed-off area which is opened to the public only after 11.00 a.m. By this time the animals will have been fed, exercised and cleaned by the livestock assistants, who are chosen for their knowledge and love of animals. During their regular exercise times, the parrots are let out to fly freely and the puppies and kittens (including Silver Tabbies and Russian Blues) can romp around. The puppies are given rides on a blanket and are only returned to their spacious cages when they are so exhausted that they will quickly fall asleep. Should one of them start crying, however, an assistant will go into the pet area to play with it and comfort it. Each Sunday, and on holidays, one member of the team comes in to look after the pets. In the evenings during the week, the store's security staff and firemen always check that all is well, topping up water when necessary or giving affection.

The department also sells a range of rodents from chinchillas to fancy rats, hamsters, gerbils and lop-eared rabbits; tropical and cold-water fish; canaries and budgerigars, but perhaps its most popular and exotic pets are the colourful parrots. Hand-reared by British breeders, these magnificent birds soon become friends with the staff, gently nibbling their fingers and flying on to their shoulders.

Spotted, striped, plain or patterned – made of pure wool, raw Indian silks or Tana lawn – the bow-tie may be small, but the choice of fabrics and styles bow-ties come in, is immense. And the Harrods selection of bows to tie is possibly the largest in the world, with over **12,600** sold last year.

The one thing you will not find, however, is a clip-on bow; they simply do not look right. But this does not mean you have to tie the bow each time you wear it: **99** per cent of Harrods bows are fitted with hooks and eyes, which means that once you have tied the bow, you can wear it like a ready-made. Sales assistants will tie the bow for customers, or will demonstrate the technique for a perfect bow to those who wish to learn.

As well as stocking a large range of designer bows from Hugo Boss, Armani, Ferragamo, Hermès,

John Comfort and Pincaldi, not to mention the creations of traditional bow-tie makers Theakes and Holliday & Brown, Harrods also commissions its own bows from Jay Vantee, famed for his perfect stitching and fine finish. These come in a glorious spectrum of raw Indian silks, from daffodil yellow through to fuschia, as well as in more sober paisleys, traditional or modern tartans, fish or elephant patterns and bold, brilliant splashes of colour. With such a small piece of cloth, you can go mad without looking outré, hence the popularity of Dunford Wood's and Vicky Holton's handpainted ties and the exclusive, hand-pieced silk patchwork bows by Stefano Ricci.

But though fashion changes, and with it the demand for the fish-tailed, butterfly or large bat-wing bows, the traditional black 'Mayfair' bow remains a favourite, as does the small, white-spotted 'Winston Churchill'.

Customers faced with such a confusion of colours, shapes and styles will find Harrods sales assistants are always on hand to help choose the right tie to match a particular jacket or suit. Bows can also be ordered in the fabric of the customer's choice, with a hand-rolled handkerchief to match.

the perfect bow-tie

THE
HARRODS
KNOW-HOW

ABOVE: *Aleck Craddock*
was a much loved Managing
Director of Harrods during
the Fraser ownership.
Thirty years a Harrodian,
he was General Manager
and Assistant Managing
Director in the 70s.
OPPOSITE AND BELOW:
During his very active
administration new escalators
were installed (via the roof)
and a highly awarded
range of packaging was
introduced, designed by
Minale Tattersfield.

ALECK CRADDOCK

In 1980 Robert Midgley retired. His successor, Aleck Craddock, had been the Assistant Managing Director. Whereas both Alfred Spence and Robert Midgley had been graduates of the House of Fraser, Aleck Craddock was a Harrodian through and through, having worked in the store for much of his life. His style was very different from his predecessors. It was more democratic and consultative. Without being in the least indecisive, Craddock paid great attention to the opinions of those about him.

With his gentlemanly manner and razor-sharp business brain, he brought an eminently practical approach to his job. He had a clear idea of what Harrods represented. 'There is a danger of being thought of as snooty, the top people's store,' he once said. 'Not by me; I never call it that because I think of it as everybody's store . . . It's all about show business — colour, style and moving trends.'

In fact, this had always been true of Harrods, at least since the days of the first Richard Burbidge. But the full possibilities of show business in Harrods were not to be realized until the reins were taken by Mohamed Al Fayed, who often stated his belief that theatre was the essence of retailing.

'HARRODS MAJOR PROJECT'

During his term of office, Aleck Craddock conceived the idea and saw through to fruition the 'Harrods Major Project': an ambitious scheme to develop the Hans Road end of the store and the fourth floor.

The west side of the building, along Hans Road, had always been the least profitable, with a very sparse customer flow. This was largely because it was served by a single lift. At the beginning of the 1980s, the only escalators in Harrods were on the other side of the store, and they dated from before the Second World War. The 'Harrods Major Project' envisaged the installation of a new set of escalators at Door No. 10 to Hans Road. These would make the whole of that side of the store more accessible. On the ground floor the Food Halls were to be extended, with a new self-service Pantry on the lower ground floor. The western end of the fourth floor, where the Management Offices had been relocated to make room for the Olympic Way, would be opened up. The offices would be moved again — to the floor above — and the vacated space redesigned as a selling area.

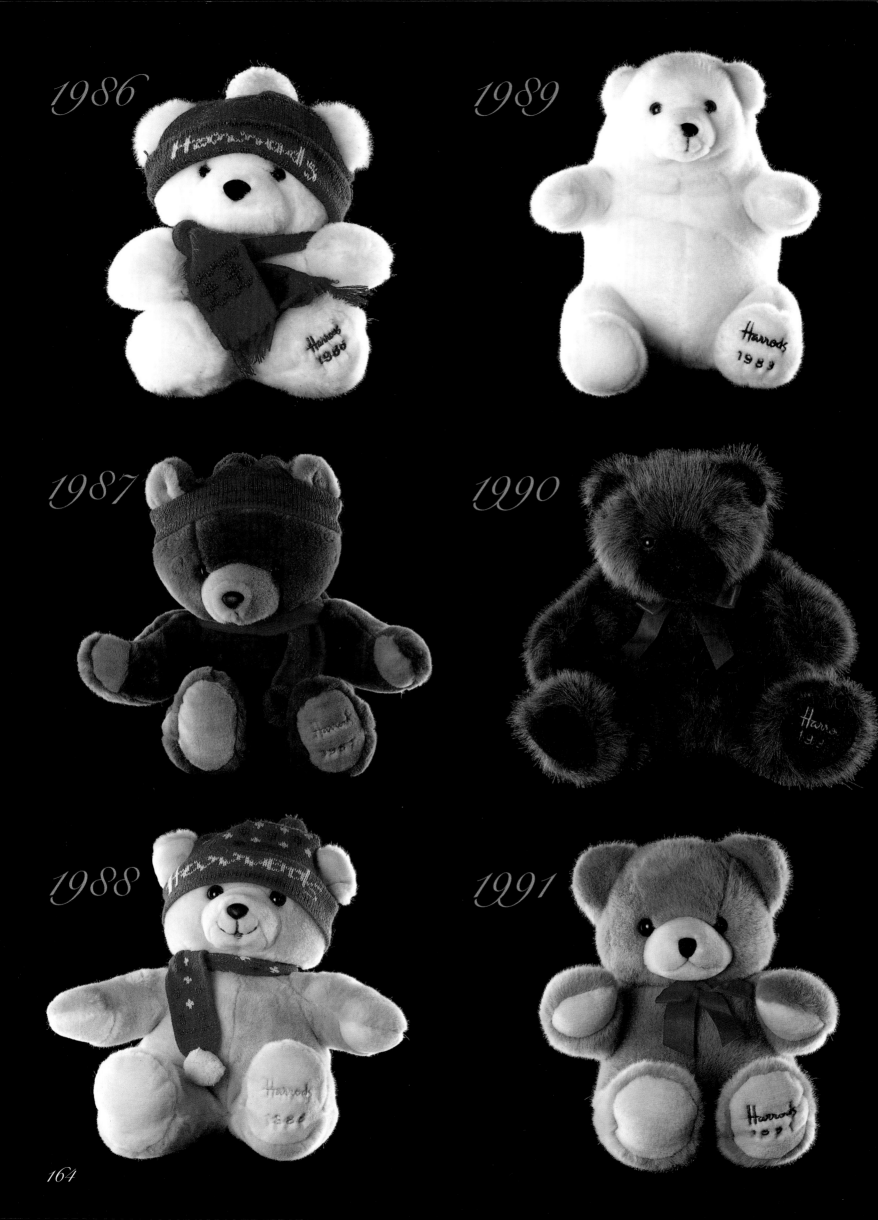

1986

1989

1987

1990

1988

1991

1992

1995

1993

1994

By 1981, a year after his appointment, Aleck Craddock was able to preside over the inauguration of the new layout. The fourth floor now also housed one of Harrods' most celebrated and successful departments — toys.

HARRODS FOR CHILDREN

Toys, and children's merchandise generally, have always been, and remain, a prime concern of the store. Harrods has always known that children who get to know the store at an early age are likely to become lifetime customers. Departments for children have expanded steadily through the decades, reflecting, no less than other areas, the changing tastes of different periods. Victorian china dolls have given way to computer games; broderie anglaise and buttoned boots to jeans and trainers.

The tradition of celebrating each Christmas with a specially designed and dated new Teddy Bear was started in 1986. The bear in different sizes dominates the displays in the enchanting soft toy room during the run-up to Christmas.

Today, under the Fayeds, the children's departments flourish as never before; no less than nine departments on the fourth floor are devoted to children, from babies to teenagers.

As well as the usual children's departments, with a full range of clothes for all ages, including school uniforms, the store boasts babies' changing rooms, children's lavatories, children's hairdressing, children's furniture and party stationery.

The Toy Departments offer a magical selection of goods. In the past at Harrods, as at other stores, they were a seasonal phenomenon. They would expand spectacularly before Christmas, but were less prominent during the rest of the year. Today the Toy Departments are spectacular all year round.

Of course Christmas is still a special time and the Christmas Toy Fair is one of the store's long-standing traditions. Since 1985, Christmas has become an even more magical time at Harrods. It is planned months in advance and has developed into a major operation involving a small army of sales staff, packers, query clerks and supervisors. A buyer is despatched, months before, to the Far East, in search of ever more imaginative decorations. In recent years new Christmas traditions have been introduced, such as the annual limited-edition Harrods teddy bear.

Every year Santa Claus leaves the North Pole to take up temporary residence in the store. But where his annual arrival used to be an ordinary enough event, now it has become a spectacular occasion, with traffic in Knightsbridge being brought to a standstill as a colourful procession precedes Santa Claus in his horse-drawn coach.

RIGHT: *Early shopping catalogues show that children have long been a focus for the store.*
BELOW: *Father Christmas arrived rather more quietly in 1932. These days he comes ceremoniously by horse-drawn carriage to take up residence in his grotto.*

166

HARRODS NEWS NOVEMBER 12TH 1928

A Million Toys for Girls and Boys!

HARRODS NEWS

Monday, Nov. 14, 1927

"Oh, what a Joyland is TOYLAND!*"*

HARRODS NEWS

January 31st, 1927.

WEE FOLKS' NUMBER

HARRODS NEWS

DEC. 9TH 1929

*'O where is my Mummy,
O where can she be?
I'm lost in Harrods and
it's time for tea.'
Parents can rest assured that
the Lost Children's service
will take good care of those who
have gone astray, and on
the Fourth Floor, whether
in search of style or discovering
new toys, no child
is disappointed.*

Since 1985, Harrods has had special shops within the store exclusively selling its own lines of merchandise. Products of popular appeal were sold first, but later the scope has widened to include men's and ladies' wear. Goods have to reach a very high specification to be given the store label. In 1995, Harrods World, a whole new store within the store, was established on the fourth floor, selling every kind of Harrods own-label merchandise.

HARRODS SHOPS AND HARRODS INTERNATIONAL

Another of the new fourth floor departments of the 1980s which was to prove very successful was the Harrods Shop. Its success was quite unexpected; perhaps the Harrods management had not fully appreciated the cachet of a Harrods label.

Having a modest selling place to fill, the management decided to move up some merchandise from the ground floor. Plastic bags and aprons in the store's colours of green and gold, and carrying the Harrods logo, had been selling rather well down there. What was meant to be a temporary measure thrived spectacularly. Within a year the Harrods Shop was taking over £1 million annually. There are now several Harrods Shops throughout the store.

Much of the success of the Harrods Shop was due to the continuing tourist boom. To be seen carrying a Harrods bag in Sydney or drinking from a Harrods mug in San Francisco was considered the height of chic. This, plus a court battle in the United States in which Harrods successfully restrained the use of its logo, led the management to decide that the store should establish an international presence. In 1983 the first satellite Harrods Shop was opened in the Nihombashi department store in Tokyo, the flagship store of the Mitsukoshi group. In the same year a small Harrods Shop was installed on the Cunard liner QE2.

ROYAL RECOGNITION

Harrods has always cherished its long association with the British royal family. These years of service were officially recognised in 1981, when Aleck Craddock, as Chairman and Managing Director, was made a Lieutenant of the Royal Victorian Order, an honour in the personal gift of Queen Elizabeth II. It was Aleck Craddock who escorted Princess Anne when she opened the refurbished and extended Food Halls in 1983. For a man who had started his career in the Food Halls, the royal inauguration was a proud moment.

Craddock's five years, from 1980 to 1985, were the store's most successful trading years yet. Sales doubled and in 1984 there came, as a crowning glory, the Queen's Award for Export Achievement.

BOARDROOM BATTLES

This award was all the more remarkable, considering that affairs
in the board room during this period were anything but tranquil.
Throughout the early 1980s Harrods was being rocked by a
mammoth ownership struggle. A second, more prolonged, 'Battle
of Knightsbridge' was raging.

By 1980 it was apparent that Sir Hugh Fraser's
hold on the House of Fraser was slipping. As it slipped,
so the international company Lonrho plc, led by its Chairman,
Tiny Rowland, was building up a stake in the company.

The end of the feud.
Tiny Rowland and
Mohamed Al Fayed
shake hands in the Food
Halls, October 1993.

By the end of 1980 his holding was just under 30 per cent. At a dramatic board meeting in January 1981, Sir Hugh Fraser was replaced as Chairman of the House of Fraser by Professor Roland Smith. This was immediately followed by a bid from Tiny Rowland for outright control of the company, which was opposed by the newly-installed Smith. The proposed take-over was passed to the Monopolies and Mergers Commission where, after consideration, it was blocked.

But the battle did not end there. In a protracted struggle with the House of Fraser, Lonrho issued several more proposals. But Professor Smith held firm. Thwarted, Tiny Rowland decided to get rid of his holding in the House of Fraser. In October 1984 he sold it to Alfayed Investment and Trust (UK) plc.

In March 1985 Mohamed Al Fayed, with his two brothers, made a cash offer for the remaining equity of the group. It was accepted and the purchase went through. The total deal amounted to a £615 million outright purchase. This turned the House of Fraser into a private company. Of more importance to Harrods, it turned the store into a family business once again, for the first time since Charles Digby Harrod sold his shop in 1889. Mohamed Al Fayed became Chairman, with his brother Ali as his deputy. They quickly made it clear that they would not be absentee owners interested only in the balance sheet as an indication of their store's prosperity and progress. Mohamed established his office in the store, while his brother is based in the Mayfair headquarters of the parent company, Harrods Holdings plc. Both are personally involved in the day-to-day running of the business. (In 1994, when the decision was made to float the House of Fraser as a public limited company, the Fayeds chose to keep Harrods as their private family company.)

For many years, Tiny Rowland kept up a relentless, very public, but unsuccessful, campaign to wrest the store from Mohamed Al Fayed. An amusing legacy of this battle was a twelve-foot-long stuffed shark labelled 'Tiny', which hung for years in Harrods fish department, until it was finally lowered by Mr Rowland in a gesture of surrender in 1993. The feud was over: Tiny Rowland and Mohamed Al Fayed, both smiling broadly, shook hands. A year later, the shark was auctioned for £4500 in aid of the charity Childline.

CHAPTER

6

HARRODS TODAY

A detail from the Egyptian Hall created by Mohamed Al Fayed in 1991. The sculpture and frieze are inspired by the art of the 19th Dynasty in Ancient Egypt.

The famous Harrods motto, *Omnia Omnibus Ubique*, 'Everything for Everybody Everywhere', is not an exercise in hyperbole; it is a simple statement of fact. Since the 1890s the store has dedicated itself to supplying goods and services, no matter how unusual, to whomsoever might want them, and to anywhere in the world. Service, both in the store and beyond, has always been a prime concern of Harrods. That other celebrated motto, also coined over a century ago — 'Harrods Serves the World'— is as true today as it ever was.

Sind Sie bei Harrods angestellt?
ハロッズで働いているんですか?
do you work at Harrods?
usted trabajas para Harrods?
ハロッズで働いているんですか?
ッズで働いているんですか?
you work at Harrods?

LEFT: *Three of the Harrods Green Men who welcome visitors to the store, with the question they are most commonly asked.*

This service starts at each of the store's eleven main doors. Outside the main entrances stand the well-known Green Men, the commissionaires in their smart green, brass-buttoned uniforms, with peaked caps in summer and top hats in winter. Until fairly recently, they were required to be over 6 foot 3 inches tall. They must still, however, be men of great diplomacy and unfailing good humour with an encyclopaedic knowledge of the store and an ability to spot and summon a taxi within seconds. Despite having the word 'Harrods' emblazoned on the cap of his distinctive uniform, remarks one Green Man wryly, the most frequent question he is asked is, 'Do you work at Harrods?'

The greatest burden of service, of course, falls on the staff within the store. From the girl at the information desk who smilingly answers the same question twenty or thirty times a day, to the man who calculates exactly how much curtaining you will require, this vast army of assistants is there to meet the customer's needs. Estimates of the number of people working at Harrods vary. At present, it is generally put at 4000, rising to 4500 during Christmas and sale times. But the matter is complicated by the fact that not all the employees are full-time and that some additional staff are supplied by various concessions within the store, such as the stands in the Perfumery Department. This means that, at times, there are nearly 6000 people working at Harrods.

Recruitment is continuous; assistants are constantly joining or leaving. The permanent recruitment team must keep track of vacancies, place advertisements, deal with applications and interview applicants. Approximately 24,000 people apply for jobs each year; of these, as many as 12,000 are interviewed, and 2000 may be engaged.

Having been accepted, the new recruit becomes the responsibility of the training department. He or she is introduced into the customer care programme. Although a more egalitarian society has done away with the old exaggerated deference towards customers, the staff must remain polite, helpful, long-suffering and knowledgeable. They must also be well turned-out. Harrods has various training schemes. The main ones are the 'career training scheme' for school-leavers and young people up to twenty years of age, and the 'executive training scheme' for graduates and internal candidates training to be supervisors. Standards for this last scheme are very high and the competition fierce.

Amongst the most important members of staff are the buyers, the men and women in each department, who are responsible for choosing the merchandise to be sold. Quality is paramount at Harrods. If it sometimes seems that merchandise is dearer than at other stores, this is because the goods must always be of a superlative quality. Harrods buyers travel the world to ensure that the store's high standards — not only of material and manufacture but also of fashion — are met. To become a Harrods buyer is the dream of every ambitious applicant. But many years may pass, and many stages be gone through, before that applicant finally finds himself or herself selecting glass and china at an Italian trade fair, or as a fully-fledged fashion buyer at a prêt à porter in Paris.

CENTRE: *The staff in the fish department are artists as well as experts in their trade. Every day with assured taste, they display their wares in a perfect harmony of colour,*

AT THE CUSTOMER'S SERVICE

However, attending to the needs of the public on the shop floor is merely one of the many services provided by Harrods. Others include a tax-free shopping and export bureau, Harrods bank, a theatre ticket agency, a travel bureau and luxury coach tours. There is a lost property office, a lost children section and dry-cleaning service with laundry, mending, alterations and shoe-repairing. Harrods will monogram your shirts or pyjamas, make your curtains and upholstery, or provide you with a complete interior design service. There is a Barber Shop, a Hair and Beauty Salon and a Children's Hairdressers. At the Executive Service Suite on the first floor, today's executive women can go for advice on dress.

For gastronomes there is the Harrods Hamper Service. The Gift and Bridal Registry brings Harrods expertise to the organizing of a wedding gift list.

Places to eat range from the elegant Georgian Restaurant, to the Bar Fromage with its wide range of cheeses, the Champagne and Oyster Bar and the Deli. There is even a pub, 'The Green Man', rich in the ambience of a traditional English hostelry, while for more health-conscious customers there is the Health Juice Bar, which first opened in 1954. Lately, a Sushi Bar and a Pizzeria have been added to create a more international range of eating places.

LEFT: *The denizen of the deep, the Manager of the subterranean Safe Deposit. Customers must give their password before entering.*
BELOW: *This late-nineteenth century installation still has on its frosted glass doors the monogram of the early company: HSL, for Harrods Stores Ltd.*
RIGHT: *The original advertisement for the services of the Safe Deposit.*

The behind-the-scenes activity is no less vital for efficient customer service. On the fifth floor are the Central Cash Office and the Accounts Bureau. Over a million transactions are generated by almost 210,000 account customers each year. Across Brompton Road, in the Trevor Square building, is the busy telephone exchange.

Harrods pioneered telephone shopping at the beginning of the century, and today many orders are placed by telephone through the telephone/mail order department at Osterley.

Co-ordinating the store's relations with its customers is the all-important Customer Service section, which deals with personal callers, handles the mass of incoming and outgoing mail, re-directs complaints, compliments and queries to the appropriate departments, and looks after the documentation of all goods being exported by sea or air freight.

SAFE DEPOSIT

One survival of the store's Victorian services is the famous Safe Deposit, which was inaugurated in 1896. This 'Temple of Safety' or 'Citadel of Security' was built of impregnable steel,

on the principle applied to the construction of armour-plated battle ships. Its safes and strong rooms guaranteed complete safety and secrecy. It was entirely fire-proof. Replete with steel bars, drill-proof doors, unpickable locks, mahogany fittings and frosted glass, it is the one area of the store that remains unchanged. It still houses deposits of immense value; no questions are ever asked. Its atmosphere is one of an impenetrable, underground dungeon. On being once asked how he could possibly bear to remain, day after day, in this claustrophobic atmosphere, the manager gave a perfectly reasonable answer: 'I used to be a sub-mariner.'

Nº 4

CENTRE: *Queen Elizabeth leaving Harrods with the two Princesses, Elizabeth and Margaret Rose, 1938. The royal family have patronised the store since the beginning of the century.*

CLOCKWISE FROM TOP RIGHT: *Queen Alexandra; Queen Mary; Queen Maud of Norway; the ever majestic Queen Mary, 1951; Queen Elizabeth II with Mr Al Fayed at the Windsor Horse Show which Harrods sponsors; Queen Elizabeth with Princess Margaret, c. 1949.*

The new Osterley Distribution and Administration Centre; a switch from manual to computer control.
OPPOSITE: *The impressively high storage stacks.*
THIS PAGE: *Phases of the dispatch and delivery service.*

NEW TECHNOLOGY

The new owners' commitment to keeping Harrods in the forefront of retail technology was demonstrated in 1989, when the warehousing facilities at the old Barnes Depository were superseded by a new distribution centre at Osterley in Middlesex. Rivalling Harrods itself in size and costing £30 million, the centre is one of the most advanced in the world. In its massive warehouse are stored over four million items of stock which are stacked and retrieved by computerized trolleys. The site also provides accommodation for several administrative offices which had been taking up valuable selling space in Knightsbridge.

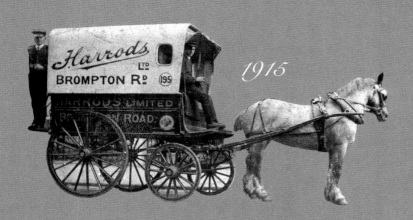

1915

1905

Delivery vans and their slogans from 1905 to the present day.

1919

1937

1907

1947

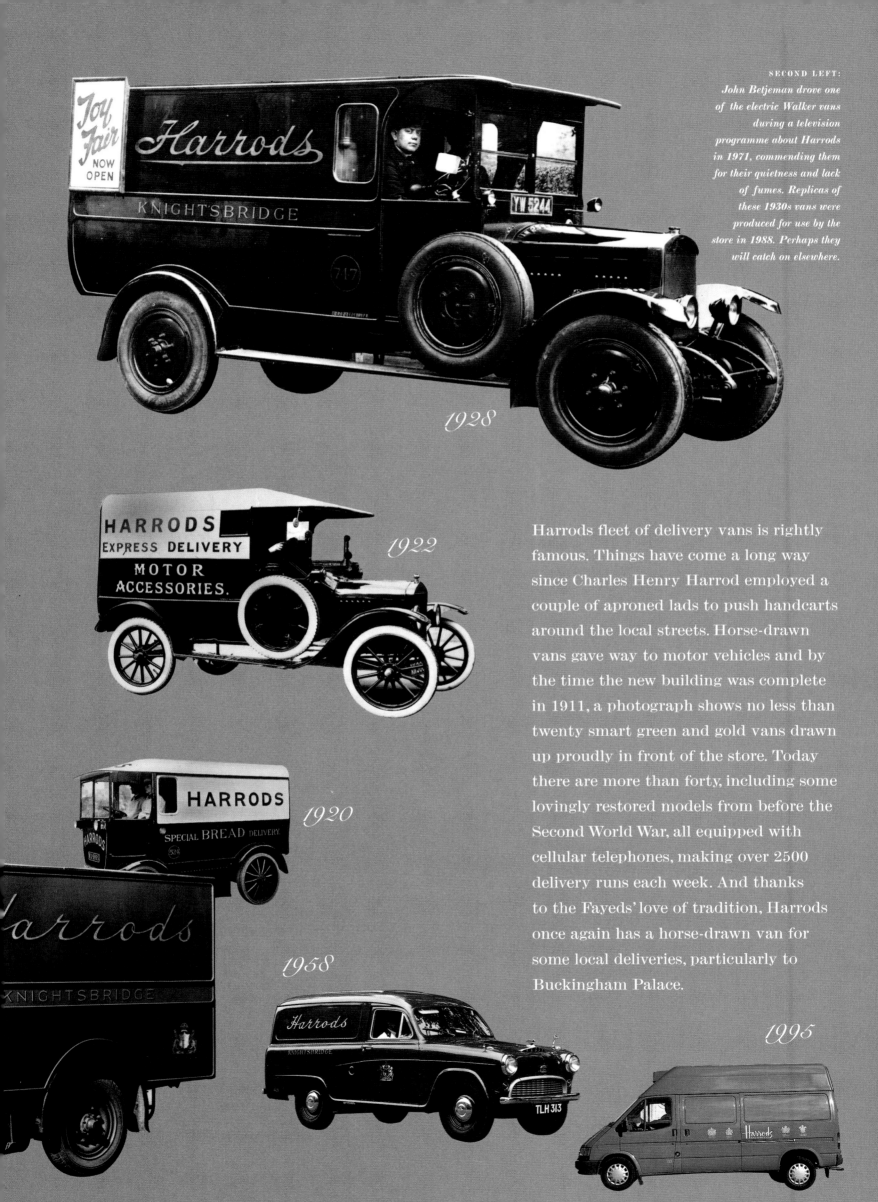

1928

1922

1920

1958

1995

Harrods fleet of delivery vans is rightly famous. Things have come a long way since Charles Henry Harrod employed a couple of aproned lads to push handcarts around the local streets. Horse-drawn vans gave way to motor vehicles and by the time the new building was complete in 1911, a photograph shows no less than twenty smart green and gold vans drawn up proudly in front of the store. Today there are more than forty, including some lovingly restored models from before the Second World War, all equipped with cellular telephones, making over 2500 delivery runs each week. And thanks to the Fayeds' love of tradition, Harrods once again has a horse-drawn van for some local deliveries, particularly to Buckingham Palace.

The Export Despatch Department, where goods are expertly packed to be sent to all corners of the world, is equally famous. It is here that one appreciates just how thoroughly Harrods does 'serve the world'. This export trade is worth many millions of pounds a year. In its time, the store has despatched everything, from the most mundane to the most bizarre. A handkerchief, costing 35 pence, has been sent to Los Angeles, by air, at a cost of £17.50. Harrods is much appreciated by homesick expatriates. Alfred Hitchcock, for example, used to arrange to have clotted cream sent out to him in Hollywood. A gazebo has been dispatched to one Arab sheikh, and the replica of a 1901 Ford to another. Leka, the son of King Zog of Albania, once instructed Harrods to send a 700-pound baby elephant to California as a token of his admiration of the State Governor, Ronald Reagan. Understandably, the Governor donated it to the Sacramento Zoo.

LEFT AND BELOW:
The frighteningly delicate and valuable Baccarat Crystal Blue Tsar goblet needs to be delivered to a customer. The packaging is incredible but effective.

Clotted cream to Alfred Hitchcock, Hollywood...

...and a handkerchief, airfreighted to Los Angeles.

COSMOPOLITAN HARRODS

As Harrods continues to serve the world so, increasingly, is the world coming to Harrods to be served. It has become one of the great tourist attractions not only of London, but of the world. No less than Buckingham Palace or the Tower of London, Harrods is one of the sights of the metropolis. To visit London without visiting Harrods is unthinkable. The clientele has become progressively more international. Harrods departments are aswirl with the colourful costumes of customers from all nations of the world, and there is a corresponding babel of languages. Interpreters are usually at hand: the staff includes more than seventy nationalities. There is always a sprinkling of those unmistakably English gentlewomen who would never dream of shopping anywhere other than Harrods.

This kaleidoscopic mixture of customers, swollen by the growth of tourism and, more especially, the oil boom, has given rise to a crop of anecdotes. A saleswoman in the Perfumery Hall was asked by a wealthy Middle-Eastern customer to multiply his already astonishingly substantial order by five: one for each of his wives. An American matron flew Concorde to Heathrow, took a taxi to Harrods where she bought two suitcases which she filled in the fur department and then, shopping done, flew Concorde back to New York.

HARRODS INTERNATIONAL

The world comes to Harrods, and in recent years Harrods has also taken more and more to going out into the world. Harrods International has burgeoned in the decade following the first Japanese venture in 1983. Since the Fayeds acquired the store, new outlets have been opened at international airports: the opening of a shop at Frankfurt Airport in 1986 has been followed by London Heathrow (a tax-free shop and miniature food hall at Terminal Three and an arcade of shops at Terminal Four), Hamburg, Toronto and Vienna. Harrods International has thrived in the Far East. There are now more than twenty Harrods Shops, Food Halls and Tea Rooms in Mitsukoshi stores throughout Japan, and in 1993 a Harrods Shop was opened at the Takishamaya store in Singapore.

The decoration of many of these shops recreates in miniature the character of the Knightsbridge store, and great care has been taken to preserve the special distinction attached to the Harrods name. There still is Only One Harrods.

Motifs from Harrods packaging of the 1950s show that the store has seen itself for some time as it truly is: one of the sights of London.

THERE IS ONLY ONE SALE

Never, of course, is the mélange of people in the Knightsbridge
store more in evidence than during the world-renowned
twice-yearly sales. These have come a long way since Harrods
first advertised its 'Winter Clearance Sale' in 1894, particularly
since Mohamed Al Fayed has injected a new spirit of show
business into the occasions. He has managed to attract such
diverse celebrities as Charlton Heston, Diana Ross, Nigel Mansell,
and the Speaker of the House of Commons, Betty Boothroyd,
to perform the opening ceremony. On each occasion a generous
donation is made to a charity chosen by the guest.
The shouted countdown to the time of opening has developed
into an exciting ritual. But exciting or not, the sale always opens
dead on time: the store stands to lose over £16,000 for each
minute of trading that is lost.

It is significant that the sales are widely advertised,
not only throughout Britain, but on the Continent and in the
Middle East. The occasions are covered as avidly by the European
news media as they are locally.

Harrods Sales are at their most frantic for only the
first couple of days, but they are meticulously planned months in
advance. Extra assistants, extra cleaners, extra cash registers,
extra on-line terminal links with the head office computers of
credit card companies must be organized. And if the event is
planned with military precision, it is, frankly, against something
very like an invading army that the preparations are being made.

The great surge of customers (the keenest of whom
will have camped outside the store overnight) rampaging through
the various departments in search of china or furs, towels or
television sets, can be assured of one thing: the Harrods sale is a
genuine sale. Never does the term 'value for money' have more
validity than during these bi-annual forays. What the exhausted
shoppers stagger away with will be real bargains.

But the transaction is far from being one-sided.
On the first Saturday of a sale, it is not unusual for Harrods to
take the staggering sum of £11 million.

The first ever Harrods sale was in 1894. Today Harrods recognizes that customers must be enticed into the store by events which are exciting and fun. Since 1988, the January and July sales have been opened by a celebrity making a grand entry. The countdown to opening on the starting day is always dramatic, as these impatient twins convey.

MOHAMED AL FAYED, MERCHANDISE MAGICIAN

'Fantasy' is a word frequently on the lips of Mohamed Al Fayed, the Chairman and owner of Harrods. Fantasy, glamour, the romance of retailing — more than ever before, these are the hallmarks of Harrods today. The store still has its wealth of expertise and its commitment to quality and service. But something more has been added — a sense of occasion. In the same way that his restoration of the Paris Ritz has revived the splendour of the famous old hotel, so Mr Al Fayed has resolved to make Harrods a dazzling place, a place where shopping becomes an exciting and unique experience. If the store is to run smoothly, it needs efficient organization, and Harrods is fortunate to have an experienced and capable management team. But, as in the time of the first Sir Richard Burbidge, it is the man at the helm who sets its character and charts its future course.

Unlike many of his predecessors, Mohamed Al Fayed does not have a background in retailing, but he has a sure sense of what Harrods has always been and what he wants it to be. He is a perfectionist when it comes to putting his ideas into effect. His daily tours of the store ensure that every detail is right. Like his Edwardian predecessor, Mr Al Fayed has vision, and the determination to realize his vision. Moreover, his love of history has meant that now more than ever Harrods is aware of its fascinating past.

'Harrods,' the Chairman has said, 'is not just a money-making venture for me; it is part of Britain's heritage. It is a place which I love. Because I love it, I will ensure that it remains simply the most beautiful store in the world.'

ABOVE: *Mohamed Al Fayed, Chairman and owner of Harrods since 1985.*
LEFT: *The finely crafted chandeliers in the Fruit and Floral Hall were installed at the time of the restoration of that department in 1988.*

He has been true to his word. Never, since its Edwardian heyday, has there been so much investment in the store. In 1987, the owners set out on an ambitious £250 million programme of revival, regeneration and expansion. Restoration and refurbishment, which had already begun in the Food Halls, was extended to other departments. Boardings and fittings erected over the past half-century were torn down to reveal original features. Back into public view came those splendours of the past: Edwardian Rococo ceilings and capitals, Art Nouveau mouldings and ceramic tiles, Art Deco marble pillars, bronze grilles and wrought-iron banisters. What could not be restored was recreated, using materials and craftsmanship of exceptional quality. When the warren of passages, stockrooms and staff cloakrooms in the basement was to be converted into a new banking hall in 1989, the designs of the old Harrods Royal Exchange of 1902 were unearthed, and the fittings and fixtures copied to recapture the self-confident elegance of the Edwardian era. One of the most stunning innovations, the ceiling of the Floral Hall, with its coloured plasterwork swirls of ribbons, fruit and flowers, and its ornate chandeliers, likewise evokes the spirit of those palmy days, but in a contemporary idiom.

ABOVE AND RIGHT:
An original display case,
a fine piece of cabinet making,
designed for the Gem Room
in 1911, still in use in
Harrods today.
FAR RIGHT: *The Bakery today,*
and as it was in the twenties,
thirties and fifties.

One of Bedford Lemere's excellent 1919 photographs of the then Menswear department. At that time it occupied a restricted space on the ground floor on the Hans Crescent side of the store.

The Man's Shop has occupied a vast area, dominating the rear portion of the ground floor since 1930. This department caters for a wide spectrum of taste and deals with its customers with confidence and courtesy.

From a private mansion in the Caribbean to a one-bedroom bachelor flat in Chelsea, no project is too big or too small for the Harrods Interior Design team. With a background that ranges from providing commercial designs for hotels and offices to creating interior designs for palaces, the design team is able to provide customers anywhere in the world with the finest service.

The department will undertake to refurbish an entire house down to the very last detail – even stocking the cellar with fine wines and the fridge with food. As well as providing furniture and fittings, fabrics and wall coverings, the team will also provide colour co-ordinated table linen, glass and cutlery. They will hang paintings and arrange ornaments, so that when the client unlocks the door, absolutely everything is in place.

Before meeting the Harrods designer on site, most customers will come in to the department for an initial discussion. This is always treated with the utmost privacy and confidentiality. They will then be presented with a design survey and scheme in the form of a design board featuring the suggested fabrics, paint colours, wallpapers and furnishings. For larger projects the team will prepare a three-dimensional mood board, richly layered with a variety of samples.

While many customers will choose furnishings and fittings available within the store, the team can also source goods internationally, and when requested they will also design and commission one-off fabrics or carpets from Harrods suppliers. Special projects, such as the painting of a mural, will also be arranged, and the team can also provide garden furniture, house plants and silk landscaping. One such project for a private sports facility in a large country house included decorating a pool hall designed in the style of a Roman temple with urns and cascading silk ivy.

the perfect room

From Melbourne to Moscow, and from Paris to Peking, the Executive Suite offers customers around the world the chance to shop at Harrods at the touch of a button.

Where possible, customers are initially invited to meet their personal sales consultant over coffee, in elegantly furnished private rooms on the first floor. During this meeting the consultant will discuss the customer's tastes and lifestyle to build up a detailed personal profile, which is then stored confidentially on computer. From then on, whenever they wish to order goods of any kind, customers need only telephone their personal consultant.

The Executive Service is popular with people who value the advice of a personal fashion stylist. For a customer wishing to build up a wardrobe or select a range of outfits for a new job or social engagement, the consultant will help to co-ordinate colours, designs and fashions appropriate to the client and the occasion. Designer separates or items from the International Room and Dress Rooms can be brought to the customer in a private dressing room. This is a service particularly popular with celebrities who prefer to shop in seclusion and with complete and total discretion.

In time, customers build up friendly, confidential relationships with their consultants, who will, if required, telephone to let them know when new designs become available. Some customers indeed, never come into the store at all, but communicate entirely by telephone or fax. At the press of a button they can order gifts – a piece of china or a bottle of champagne – to be sent, with a personal card, to friends or relatives anywhere in the world.

THE
HARRODS
KNOW-HOW

SAFEGUARDING THE ARCHITECTURAL HERITAGE

Equally important — though unseen by the general public — has been the construction work undertaken to strengthen and preserve the old fabric. The Edwardian structure was never intended to support crowds in the numbers that now throng the store, and after nearly a century it is not surprising that the building is showing signs of age.

The Fayeds realized that if their ambitious plans for Harrods were to be fulfilled, the structure had to be made sound. The steel framework, which was badly corroded, is in the process of being repaired and reinforced. Crumbling terracotta details have been restored or replaced with newly-made replicas. The famous dome, which was in danger of collapse, has been meticulously repaired. At the same time expert architectural conservators began the delicate operation of cleaning the London grime from the terracotta frontages.

Safety is always of importance. Three new staircases have had to be built to meet rigorous fire regulations; but they are far from utilitarian. In the Harrods of today, even the fire stairs are lined in marble, with intricate iron banisters.

Meanwhile the machinery which keeps the store running has been brought up to date. New turbines have been installed in the engine rooms in the main store and Trevor Square, to replace old equipment and meet increasing energy needs.

OPPOSITE: *A Baroque church in Rome? The back view of the central dome seen across the five-acre roof site.* RIGHT: *One of the chimneys on the roof.* THIS PAGE AND OVERLEAF: *Cartouches, mouldings, pediments, carvings and decorative urns were all cleaned and restored to their original crispness of outline in the refurbishment process, 1994-95.*

In 1988, additional selling space was required in the store. The Lower Ground Floor was taken over, first with a Banking Hall, later more services and departments were added along the front of the site.

The most visited area of Harrods naturally is the Ground Floor. The Food Halls, are always worth exploration both for the gourmet and the aesthete. The fragrances of the cosmetic and perfumery halls are of a different and delightful order. As might be expected accessories such as jewellery and leather goods are to be found here.
To entice the more half-hearted male shopper, the Man's Shop is just inside the Basil Street door for easy access.

*The First Floor is devoted to Ladies'
Fashions: from the International
Designer Room to lingerie, and from
swimwear to hats. There is a Bridal
Room where the fitments simply
overflow with gowns ready for future
brides to select and have made to order.*

*Furniture in many styles and periods,
antiques, furnishing fabrics, and the
Interior Design Service find their place
on the Third Floor with an art gallery,
photographic studio, carpets, pianos
and the latest sound and vision
equipment.*

*The Second Floor deals in small
household goods: so the cookshop,
tableware and bed linen are all to be
found there, together with some more
assorted items such as travel goods,
books, pets and haberdashery.*

*The Fourth Floor is the children's floor
catering for all their needs from birth
until they feel they are too grown-up
even for Way In. The Georgian
Restaurant retains its position
on this cheerful level with
alongside, the Terrace Bar,
opened in 1990, which
girdles the roofline of the
building on the Hans
Road side.*

*Apart form the sanctum of the hair
and beauty salon, the Fifth Floor
retailing area is devoted to sport in all
its forms. The rest of the space on
that floor is discreetly taken up by
administration.*

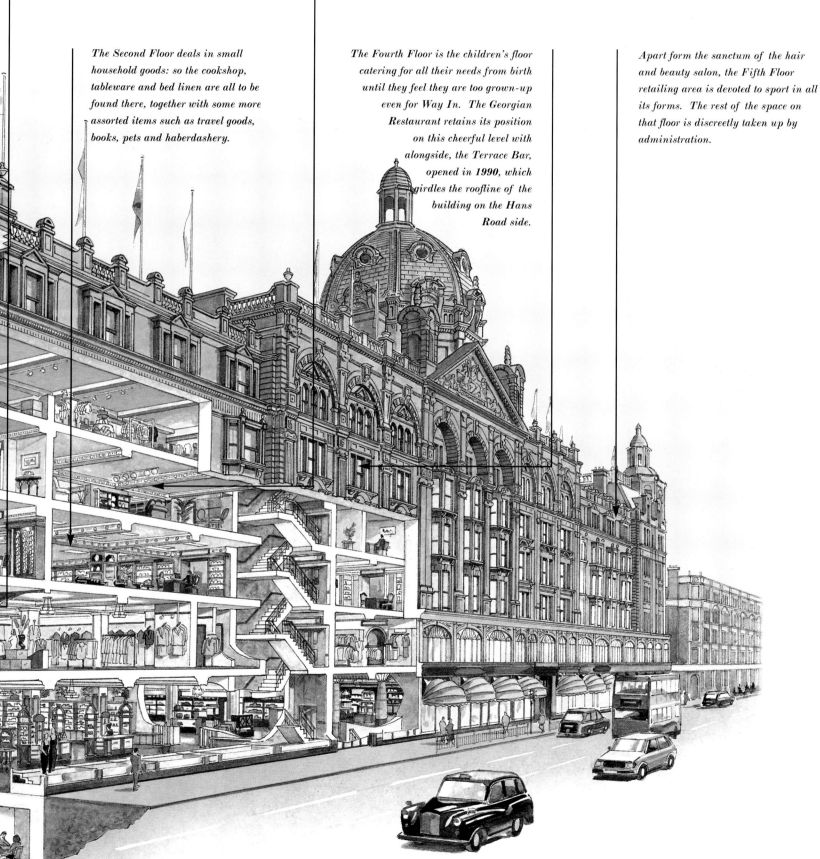

HARRODS 1995

Rationalization means that each floor has a distinct character and type of merchandise.

TRANSFORMATION

There is hardly a corner of the store which has not been touched by the current refurbishment programme. One of the first interiors to receive attention was the Leather Room on the ground floor, now restored to its elegant between-the-wars décor, with beautiful veneered display cases made to match those remaining from the 1920s. The Man's Shop has been given an entirely new layout, giving a feeling of space and relaxation. A lavish new Jewellery Room has been created, whose white and gold opulence, lit by glittering crystal chandeliers, recalls the splendour of Harrods' famous, but long-vanished Gem Room.

Some departments stand out among the many to receive special attention. The selling area has been extended to the fifth floor, where a new sports and leisure complex has been designed to replace the once revolutionary Olympic Way. On the ground floor, the new Room of Luxury features the merchandise of such celebrated names as Louis Vuitton, Les Must de Cartier, Ferragamo, Gucci, Christian Lacroix and Hermès.

On the fourth floor, Children's World (an area very close to the owner's heart) has been improved by the transfer of children's clothing from the first floor, to be integrated with the famous Toy Shop. For the first time since the 1920s all departments for children have been brought together on one floor.

This arrangement is part of a general rationalization of the layout of the store in recent years. Because of the store's complicated ground plan and sheer size, it has been easy for customers to get lost in Harrods, but today visitors to the store should have less difficulty in finding what they are looking for.

It is perhaps the ground floor and lower ground floor that have seen the most radical and romantic transformation. The new Banking Hall was merely the start. A comprehensive assessment of the selling space available in the building led to the conclusion that not only the fifth floor but also the lower ground floor had to be converted to retail use. The lower ground floor alone would give a further 33,000 square feet of selling space. A new east-west enfilade, starting at Harrods Bank, was designed to run the length of the Brompton Road frontage through a series of customer service areas and new departments. At its centre is the lower level of the amazing Egyptian Halls.

What have playing cards, a plate, shoehorn, pen and a wallet in common? They are all goods of superlative quality available in the International Room of Luxury. Within this department, on the ground floor of Harrods, is the site of the original modest little grocer's shop.

*The Egyptian Halls were designed
and installed to stimulate an interest
in Egyptian art and life. They express
the same extravagant spirit as the
French Rococo decoration chosen by the
first Burbidge. The Halls display an
arresting collection of beautiful and
curious objects, old and new.*

BOTTOM: *Replica head of Rameses II.* TOP RIGHT AND BELOW: *Lighting design of a high quality, creating a special ambience.* LEFT TO RIGHT: *Three sections of the wall frieze from the tomb of Rameses II, showing the cycle of life, from birth to death.* BOTTOM RIGHT: *Replica figure of a Chinese soldier from an Imperial tomb. Modern glass artefacts, before a column depicting an early Egyptian glass blower.*

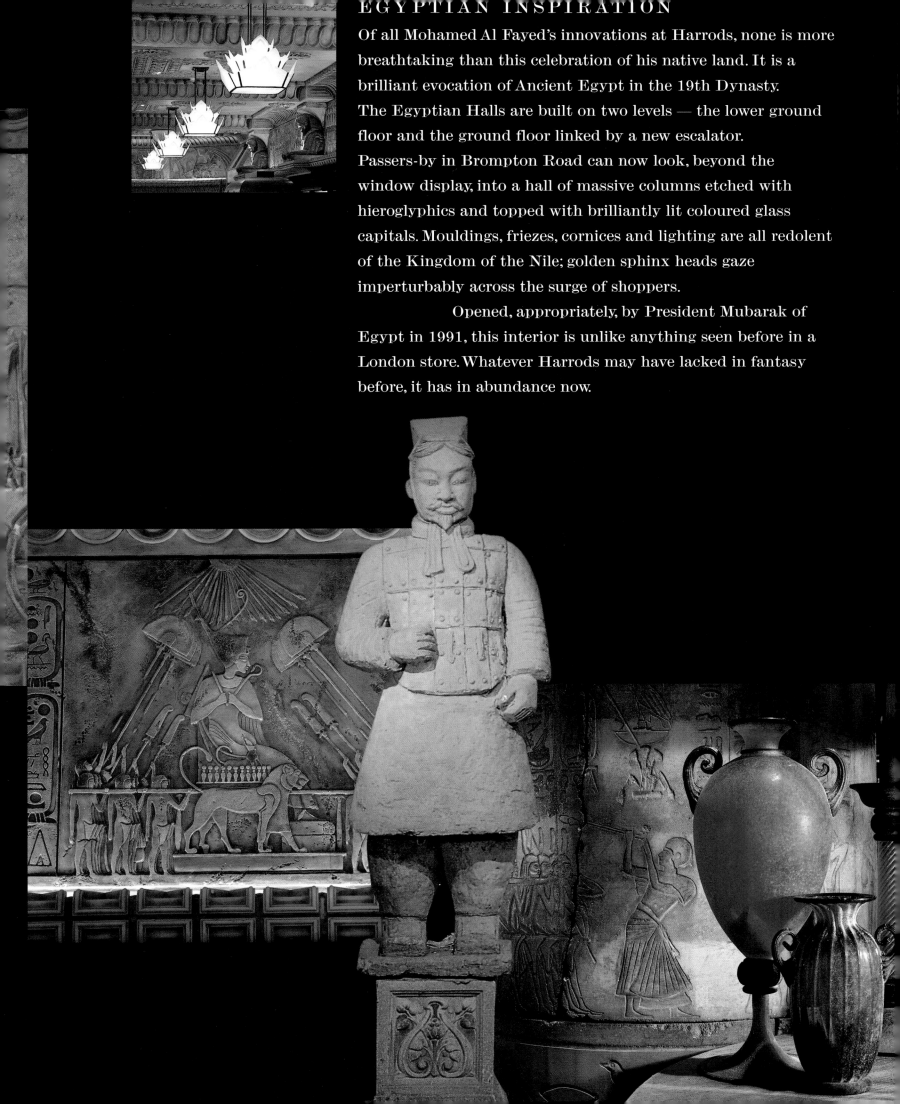

EGYPTIAN INSPIRATION

Of all Mohamed Al Fayed's innovations at Harrods, none is more breathtaking than this celebration of his native land. It is a brilliant evocation of Ancient Egypt in the 19th Dynasty. The Egyptian Halls are built on two levels — the lower ground floor and the ground floor linked by a new escalator. Passers-by in Brompton Road can now look, beyond the window display, into a hall of massive columns etched with hieroglyphics and topped with brilliantly lit coloured glass capitals. Mouldings, friezes, cornices and lighting are all redolent of the Kingdom of the Nile; golden sphinx heads gaze imperturbably across the surge of shoppers.

Opened, appropriately, by President Mubarak of Egypt in 1991, this interior is unlike anything seen before in a London store. Whatever Harrods may have lacked in fantasy before, it has in abundance now.

PANACHE

The same panache is evident in all the Chairman's projects. The elegant Harrods delivery van, drawn by black Friesian horses, has already been mentioned. It is to be seen bowling daily through the streets of Knightsbridge. Harrods carriages are a regular feature of the Windsor Horse Show (which is sponsored by the store).

The Chairman's love of Scotland has also left its mark on the store. To the surprise and delight of customers, kilted pipers are often to be found parading through the various departments. Harrods now has a tartan, which was much in evidence during the 1994 'Highland Christmas'.

Mr Al Fayed was not the first to think of illuminating the outside of the store with electric lights; the idea originated as a Christmas decoration in 1959. However, he has greatly increased the number of bulbs, to nearly 15,000, and the store is now lit up, not just at Christmas, but in the evenings throughout the year. It is very much in tune with the Chairman's sense of the dramatic that the sight of Harrods, dazzlingly illuminated like some great liner out at sea, remains one of the delights of night-time Knightsbridge.

The tartan in the background and worn by the pipers belongs to the Clan Ross. The sight and sound of the advancing pipers is sometimes a source of amazement to shoppers who have never heard bagpipes played before.

217

FUTURE PROJECTS

Harrods has never remained static; it must always be looking
to the future. Following the completion of the giant new
distribution centre at Osterley, there is talk of a second Osterley
building. In the search to make use of all available space near
the main Knightsbridge building, the Harrods car park in
Brompton Place is being redeveloped to provide extra parking
and new offices. And there are plans for building an extra
storey for Administration, Advertising and Display on the roof
of the store itself.

Most ambitious of all is the project to convert the
old warehouse and dispatch building in Trevor Square into the
luxurious Harrods House Hotel. This would involve a £150
million investment programme. The family already owns the
most famous hotel in the world, the Hôtel Ritz in the Place
Vendôme in Paris, where the refurbishment programme has

*Mohamed Al Fayed,
Chairman of Harrods
does not stand on ceremony
and likes to have a go at
many of the activities
around the store.
(President Hosni
Mubarak of Egypt came
to Harrods in 1991 to open
the Egyptian Halls.)*

A DAY IN THE LIFE
OF A HARRODIAN

10.00 a.m.
The 'Green Men' at
store opening

11.00 a.m.
Cooking in the
Kitchens

12.00 a.m.
Throwing dough in
the Pizzeria

12.30 p.m.
Entertaining young
customers

created an atmosphere of unrivalled luxury and glamour.
It is some measure of the Chairman's vision and courage that,
in a period of deep recession, he has been able to contemplate
this programme of continuing and spectacular expansion.
In 1999, at the end of the twentieth century, Harrods will
celebrate its one hundred and fiftieth anniversary; it will
celebrate it in the certain knowledge that it is now stronger,
bigger and more vibrant than it has ever been.

Standing in the Room of Luxury on the ground
floor of Harrods, it is difficult to appreciate that this is the very
spot where, almost a century and a half ago, Charles Henry
Harrod stood on the sawdust-strewn floor of his one-room shop,
selling packets of loose tea and bars of yellow soap.

'Harrods,' Mr Al Fayed recently claimed,
'will be here for ever.' How astonished and delighted Mr Harrod
would be to hear it.

5.30 p.m.
A final helping hand

2.30 p.m.
Entertaining visiting
dignitaries

4.00 p.m.
Working in
the Meat Hall

1.00 p.m.
Assisting in the
Man's Shop

ABOVE: *The College of Arms granted this armorial to Harrods in 1991.*
OVERLEAF: *Harrods by night with its 15,000 bulbs alight looks like a gallant transatlantic liner moored by chance in Knightsbridge.*

ACKNOWLEDGEMENTS

This book would not have been possible without the help of the staff of many departments of Harrods. Our special thanks go to those working in the Food Halls, who were unfailingly helpful despite the disruption caused by our photography, and the staff of the stables, in particular David West.

We are grateful to the following for sharing their Harrods know-how: Raj Assinand (china), Steve Agyepong (fish), Martin Wick (cheese), David Whacket (antiques), Terry Davies (pianos), Tracey Hemus (interior design), Julia Eccles (executive service), Colin Missenden (saddles), Myfanwy Morgan (pets), Georgina Kelly (bow-ties).

For their assistance in the making of this book we are particularly grateful to the Harrods Company Archives (Nadene Hansen) and the Press Office (Vanessa Green).

Photographs by Fritz von der Schulenburg: pages 2–3, 4, 5, 8, 11, 16–17, 20–1, 22–3, 24–5, 26, 27, 30–1, 32–3, 36–7 (people), 42, 44 (below), 67, 75, 76–7, 124–5, 168, 169, 174, 176, 178–9 (below), 180, 181 (below), 184, 185, 187 (below right), 188, 192–3, 194, 196–7 (below), 200–1, 204, 205, 206–7, 212–13, 214–15, 216–17 (pipers), 222–3, 224.

Photographs by Stuart Duff: pages 13, 14, 15, 18, 29, 34–5, 36–7 (clock), 45, 46–7 (below), 47(top), 48 (below), 49, 50, 51, 57, 58, 60–1, 82, 84, 85, 86 (below), 93, 100, 106, 108, 110–11, 120–1, 121, 122, 123, 130–1 (centre), 136–7, 147, 150–1, 154–5 (legs), 156–7, 160, 161, 163 (below), 164, 165, 170–1, 189, 202, 203, 210–11, 216 (tartan).

The publishers thank the following for permission to reproduce photographs: Guildhall Library, Corporation of London/Bridgeman Art Library, London, page 43; Selfridges Archive, page 95 (bottom right); Mander & Mitchenson, pages 96 (except top), 97; *The Independent*/Glynn Griffiths, page 172–3 ; Royal Commission Historical Monuments of England, pages 95 (top), 96 (top), 102–3, 104, 105, 198–9 (Bedford Lemere photographs); the Trustees of The Wedgwood Museum, Barlaston, Staffordshire, page 129 (except bottom left). The photograph on page 28 (top left) is by Max Grizaard. Other pictures are from the Harrods Archives.

The excerpt from Eric Newby's *A Traveller's Life* is reproduced by permission of HarperCollins Publishers.

The diadem (page 14) and brooch (page 29) photographed by courtesy of Kojis in Harrods Fine Jewellery. Harrods Room of Luxury merchandise (page 210) photographed by courtesy of Gucci (diary, pens, playing cards, shoe horn), Hermès (plate) and Chloë (bag).

*Dorothy Marshall is a veteran
Harrodian with fifty years' service
behind her. A few years ago she
asked the Chairman for some
new employment. At ninety-five,
she now comes once a week,
with obvious pleasure, to play
the piano in the Cosmetics Hall.*